VOID AND VOICE

VOID AND VOICE

Essays on Literary and Historical Currents

By
Kenneth Sherman

Mosaic Press
Oakville, ON - Buffalo, NY

Canadian Cataloguing in Publication Data

Sherman, Kenneth, 1950-
  Void & voice : essays on literary & historical currents

ISBN 0-88962-645-6

I. Literature – 20th century – History and criticism. I. Title. II. Title: Void and voice.

PN771.S54 1998   809'.04   C98-930576-7

No part of this book may be reproduced or transmitted in any form, by any means, electronic or mechanical, including photocopying and recording information storage and retrieval systems, without permission in writing from the publisher, except by a reviewer who may quote brief passages in a review.

Published by MOSAIC PRESS, P.O. Box 1032, Oakville, Ontario, L6J 5E9, Canada. Offices and warehouse at 1252 Speers Road, Units #1&2, Oakville, Ontario, L6L 5N9, Canada and Mosaic Press, 85 River Rock Drive, Suite 202, Buffalo, N.Y., 14207, USA.

MOSAIC PRESS, in the USA:
85 River Rock Drive, Suite 202,
Buffalo, N.Y., 14207
Phone / Fax: 1-800-387-8992
E-mail:
cp507@freenet.toronto.on.ca

MOSAIC PRESS, in Canada:
1252 Speers Road, Units #1&2,
Oakville, Ontario, L6L 5N9
Phone / Fax: (905) 825-2130
E-mail:
cp507@freenet.toronto.on.ca

MOSAIC PRESS in the UK and Europe:
DRAKE INTERNATIONAL SERVICES
Market House, Market Place,
Deddington, Oxford. OX15 OSF

Mosaic Press acknowledges the assistance of the Canada Council, the Ontario Arts Council and the Dept. of Canadian Heritage, Government of Canada, for their support of our publishing programme.

Copyright © Kenneth Sherman, 1998
ISBN 0-88962-645-6
Cover Design by: Amy Land
Book design by: Adam Sherwood
Printed and bound in Canada

*For Debbie Dempsey, Kem Luther,
and David Penhale*

CONTENTS

Preface

I

The Tailor Shop	15
Silver Braids	22
Void and Voice: Notes from Poland	27
The Master of Repetition	46

II

Primo Levi and The Unlistened-to-Story	51
Czeslaw Milosz: The Witness of Poetry	66
Schindler's List: Reel History	76
Perishing Things and Strange Ghosts: Rupert Brooke's Last Poem	87
Are We Not Men? H.G. Wells' *The Island of Doctor Moreau*	98
What The Line Was After: Joseph Brodsky's *On Grief and Reason*	105
Orpheus Descending: Tomas Tranströmer's *For The Living And The Dead*	114

III

Crackpot: A Lurianic Myth	121
A.M. Klein: Burnt Angel	128
Eli Mandel: *The Family Romance*	134
Miriam Waddington: *Apartment Seven*	140
Robin Skelton: *The Edge of Time*	145
George Faludy: Oh, Lucky Man	150

ACKNOWLEDGEMENTS

Acknowledgments are due to the following magazines where these texts first appeared:

Books In Canada, "What the Line Was After: Joseph Brodsky's *On Grief and Reason*," "Robin Skelton: *The Edge of Time*," Tomas Tranströmer's *For The Living And The Dead*

Brick, "Primo Levi and the Unlistened-to-Story"

The Dalhousie Review, "Eli Mandel: *The Family Romance*"

Descant, "Void and Voice: Notes From Poland"

The Idler, "Czeslaw Milosz: The Witness of Poetry"

Queen's Quarterly, "Are We Not Men? H.G. Wells' *The Island of Doctor Moreau*," "Perishing Things and Strange Ghosts: Rupert Brooke's Last Poem," "The Master of Repetition," "The Tailor Shop"

Viewpoints, "Miriam Waddington: *Apartment Seven*"

Waves, "*Crackpot*: A Lurianic Myth" and "George Faludy: Oh, Lucky Man"

Praised be your name, no one.
For your sake
we shall flower.
Towards
you.

— Paul Celan, "Psalm"

And emptiness turns its face to us
and whispers
'I am not empty, I am open.'

— Tomas Tranströmer, "Vermeer"

PREFACE

At first glance it may appear strange to combine H.G. Wells, Primo Levi, Rupert Brooke, Steven Spielberg, five Canadian poets, my grandmother's silver braids, and a blind beggar in the Old City of Jerusalem. When I began writing these essays, I had no intention of producing a book. But once I had re-read them, I realized that there was something, aside from what I hope is an identifiable voice, which holds them together. We are nearing the end of a murderous century and it is obvious that its ghosts have claimed me. I would prefer to have written a purer book, a book more centred on poetry and the imagination, but I have been drawn to investigate the dark characteristics of what Osip Mandelstam called, with startling prescience, "the wolfhound age."

It seems to me now that each piece was written with Clio, the Muse of History, staring down at the page. The title of the book is taken from my description of a journey to the camps and killing fields of Poland. For some, *Void and Voice* will hearken back to George Steiner's *Language and Silence*, a book that impressed me when I first read it as an undergraduate. It is a book which challenges, not only the complacency of academia, but also some of the more fixed notions we entertain about civilization and culture. It is a book that served as a moral weathervane, though given where my family had come from, my direction was most likely predetermined. Hence, my passionate reading of Primo Levi, an author whose accumulating despair was based on his observation that his words had done nothing to stem the rising tide of technological barbarism and corporate mindlessness; or my essay on *The Island of Doctor Moreau* — an attempt to answer persistently troubling questions concerning the role of the scientist in our society. In "Perishing Things and Strange Ghosts" I challenge the image we have inherited of Rupert Brooke by examining the last poem he wrote aboard his ship as it sailed toward Galilipoli. In these essays, I am interested in literature as it relates to the unfolding human predicament and in Isaac Luria's Kabbalistic notion that the void is necessary because it is that which invites creation, urging the poet to speak and fill the emptiness.

I have divided the book into three sections. Part one presents memoirs; part two contains essays on international authors. (Here I have included one essay on film: "*Schindler's List*: Reel History" seemed to complement my other work dealing with the *Shoah*. I have noted certain references and allusions in the film, which, to my knowledge, did not appear in any reviews or articles; I hope that these will help provide a clearer understanding of the film's intent.) Part three presents my work on a number of Canadian authors who have interested me.

While most of the investigations in this book were written within the last ten years, two — "Crackpot: A Lurianic Myth" and "George Faludy, Oh Lucky Man" — go back to my early association with *Waves* magazine in the mid-seventies. The commercial nature of publishing today has lessened the chances of an author finding a home for the sort of non-academic literary essay I have been writing. I therefore wish to thank the following editors who brought these various pieces into print: Boris Castel and Joan Harcourt at *Queen's Quarterly*; David Warren at *The Idler*; Karen Mulhallen at *Descant*; Gerald Owen at *Books In Canada*; Bernice Lever at *Waves*; Andy Wainwright at *The Dalhousie Review*; and Linda Spalding at *Brick*. Most of all, I want to thank Howard Aster at Mosaic Press.

To those friends named on the dedication page, a special note of gratitude. Their patience and helpfulness in reading and discussing these essays seemed unlimited; their editorial suggestions often helped bring a blurred work into focus.

I

THE TAILOR SHOP

There was a label with the words *Custom Tailored By Sherman* sewn onto the inside breast pocket of every jacket that left my grandfather's shop. The label had been created in the the '30s; it depicted a Fred Astaire top hat and cane in the upper left hand corner. Under the fluid, woven letters of *Sherman* were five horizontal lines: a music staff. And under the staff, in staid, Protestant block letters was our city's name: TORONTO. The capital *S* of my surname began with a long needle-like line before flowing into a white, serpentine script against the black background. As a boy I would stack these labels in a small box and wonder who the artist was that had created the elegant design.

My earliest memories are of my grandfather's tailor shop. For the first five years of my life my parents and I lived above Sherman Custom Tailors in a tiny apartment consisting of a living room that also served as bedroom, and a kitchen the size of a cupboard. We shared a bathroom located down the hall with another family. The building was situated at the busy intersection of College and Bathurst. Concerns over traffic led my mother to restrict my play area to the inside of the shop. This was possible because the business was divided into two sections. The front of the store was where my grandfather, my father and my uncles would greet and fit their customers. The back, where I pedaled my blue tricycle, was a mini-factory where the cutters, tailors and pressers worked.

In the back of the shop were long cutting tables and, underneath them, large cardboard cartons for the scraps of discarded cloth. There were measuring tapes and small boxes containing chalk, Gillette razor blades and pins. Garment patterns, the colour of dried blood, dangled from hooks like sides of beef. Large spools of white thread fed the black sewing machines. Most fascinating was the ancient press-iron with its long, moveable arm. I thought of the iron itself, sleek and triangular, as the head of a prehistoric pterodactyl, whose picture I had seen in a children's book on dinosaurs. The arm of the press iron was the bird's long neck. Inside the head were tiny blue tongues of flame.

In the front of the shop the cloth samples hung like drapery on both walls. If the prospective customer could not find what he was looking for there, he was shown a catalogue of samples or led into the back where bolts of cloth, stacked to the ceiling in rough wooden cribs, were unfurled at a moment's notice. Patterns: pinstripe, herringbone, hound's tooth, sharkskin, salt and pepper, tartan. And textures: tweed, hopsack, twill, worsted, serge. I recall cloth unrolled on a large table and men bent over it, bartering in harsh Yiddish.

There was a constant barrage of arguments and jokes, at times in English, at times in Yiddish, most often in a hybrid of both. In the background I heard the careful closing of shears, the ripping of thread, the hiss of the steam press, and the Gatling gun clatter of the sewing machines that made a mockery of their name — *Singer*.

There were a number of cats — restricted, as I was, to the back of the shop — with extraordinary names: *No-Neck, Shvartz Katz, Rabinovitz*. They would doze on the cutting tables or sit like a row of sphinxes atop the bolts of cloth. My father fed and cared for them. He kept a lint brush nearby to remove any of their hairs that might have adhered to the cloth. There always seemed to be a cat that had just given birth in one of the large cardboard boxes reserved for remnants and, for as long as I can remember, there was a sign in the store front window advertising the availability of kittens.

Not only did the cats have nicknames, but so did the men who worked for my grandfather: *Elbow, Noodle, The Pinhead, The Vijulator*. I know how the last got his name. One day he came excitedly into the back of the store carrying a toy carousel that he

The Tailor Shop

had bought to give his granddaughter. He turned it on and the tiny lions and horses began rotating. "It's a *vijulator*," he said, in a thick Yiddish accent. When asked why a *vijulator*, he looked astonished. "Because it *vijulates*."

I remember a group of those men, sitting around a large table, sewing by hand. One had reading spectacles perched on his small nose and resembled a mouse. Another wore a fedora tilted back on his head and had a long dark face like a horse. Each man sitting there wore a white shirt with the sleeves rolled up, and a tape measure around the neck like a prayer shawl. They communicated not only with speech, but also with their bodies: rhetorical questions posed by raising the shoulders; theories discarded with a toss of the hand; acceptance displayed by the fatalistic nodding head.

As a child consigned to an adult world, I became an observer. Yet I could not decode much of what I was witnessing and so it remained a mystery: the family squabbles, the employee politics, the intricacies of business. There was a gallery of cheesecake photographs torn from magazines that covered the entire wall above the cutting table where my Uncle Willy worked. In the mid-'50s these were relatively tame. Still my mother fretted when I pedaled my blue tricycle about that back room; she warned my father that it was improper for a young boy to see such photos. But what could anyone do? By allowing me into the shop, they had permitted me to witness aspects of the adult world, uncensored. In any event, no one bothered to take them down.

When I was six my parents followed their generation's northern exodus out of the city core. We moved to a bungalow near Lawrence Avenue, still close to Bathurst Street. The family store was no longer an extension of my home. It was a place I visited. When I was old enough to take the public transit by myself I would occasionally go down on Saturday. I would take the Bathurst bus south to Bloor, where I transferred to the Bathurst streetcar. Changing from the smoothly running bus to the rattling red trolley, I was aware of crossing into a different world: I was moving from the clean and ordered suburbs into the older, less predictable city core. The streetcar moved more slowly and stopped more often than the bus. It clanged like an exclamation and picked up more interesting passengers.

Now that I was older, I was no longer forbidden in the front of the store. I sat in the creased leather green chair by the door and watched customers walk in. Sometimes they would ask my father *"Tedke* (a Yiddish diminutive of Teddy), is that your son?" and I would be introduced. I loved the way my father and uncles harangued one another and kibitzed with the regulars who hung around the shop. There was toothless Wild Bill, who swept the floor and ran errands; muscular Marvin the delivery-boy, who could tear a Toronto white pages telephone book in half; Maxie Stern, the mortgage broker, with serious Levantine eyes who used the store as his "office" and paced nervously by the wall phone. And there was Albert, excessively thin, misshapen, who bought cloth from my father to peddle from door to door. He spoke in low tones with a German accent and wore a cheap toupee. He was a survivor of the camps and I felt guilty whenever he caught me staring at the blue numerals tattooed on his forearm.

The photographs of naked women in the back of the store had by this time become much more graphic and risqué. This change coincided with my emergence into adolescence and I felt self-conscious, standing in the back of the store and looking surreptitiously at the pictures while my father and uncles busied themselves with work. I never saw any of them look at the photographs. I know that my Uncle Willy, who was the anthologist, dutifully changed them every other month. Maybe he thought of them as wallpaper. There was, however, one photograph that he never took down. It was a black and white publicity shot of a famous stripper and was signed — "To the Sherman boys, love, Chesty."

There was a large heavy desk in the rear of the storefront, just in front of the triple-sided mirror. My father would sit there when he filled out the order sheets. Pleats or no-pleats? Cuffs or no cuffs? Western style pockets or slant? Loops for a belt or will you wear suspenders?

Into that triple-sided mirror walked a dazzling assortment of figures, most of them awkward, disproportional. Some resembled Hollywood character actors: there was an Edward G. Robinson look-alike; a Sidney Greenstreet, a Peter Lorre.

Often, stepping up to the mirror during a try-on, they would offer vague complaints:

The Tailor Shop

"Something's not right."
"What's not right?"
"I don't know. *Something.*"
Metaphysical urgencies. Ontological despair. I recall once, after a complainant stormed out, my grandfather quipped:
"Get that. A hunchback and he expects me to make him look like John Wayne."
Along the top of the front wall of my grandfather's shop was a mural which had been painted shortly after the Second World War by a recently arrived European refugee who needed a suit but had no money to pay for it. My grandfather bartered the suit for the mural. It depicted two scenes: on the far left was a strongly built man in a mocha brown double-breasted suit. He held a set of binoculars close to his wide chest. He stared into the distance with a determined expression. There was a racetrack in the background: sleek, elongated horses ridden by tenacious jockeys in billowing blouses of pastel yellow, orange, green. A homage to Degas, perhaps.

The man in the scene at the other end of the wall stood relaxed, dressed in a baby-blue suit. In the background was a beach with palm trees, lounge chairs, bathing beauties, the distant sea. His eyes shone with self-congratulatory contentment. He was either on holiday or retired to Florida at a young age.

Looking back on the mural, I wonder what it signified? Was it meant to relate a morality fable, like those flat tableaux painted on the walls of rural Italian churches depicting the teachings of Christ, or those I saw on the ceiling of a Buddhist temple in Sri Lanka, illustrating the ways of Gautama? A few years ago I saw something similar on the wall of Beijing's Museum of the Revolution showing stations in the life of Mao. Was the man with the binoculars the risk-taker, the penultimate North American man of vision — courageous, steadfast and lucky — and was the beach scene at the other end the pay-off? The faces of both men with their square jaws and handsome features seemed interchangeable. Perhaps I am reading too much into the mural, wondering if it was confirming a materialist quest? I also wonder if it wasn't doing the opposite — providing an ironic statement by an immigrant artist unable to pay for the suit he had ordered? Am I going too far in imagining that it might have presented a subtle critique of the capitalist dream, disguised as a mural advertising the latest in men's suits. I think of Goya's mocking portrait of the Spanish royal family that hung in the palace of King Charles IV, undetected by the very subjects of the artist's scorn. And I find myself wondering about the fate of this immigrant artist. Did he survive in the New World? Was he able to live a life devoted to his painting?

I had a great fondness for that mural and was disappointed years later when my father and uncles renovated the store and covered what they thought of as an outdated painting with unattractive wood panels. I hope that one day some future shop owner will uncover it. By then the mural will have taken on the authority of nostalgia. It will be considered *cool*. But even in their original state the figures had a majestic, Byzantine quality. Flat and static, they gazed out dispassionately while the less attractive customers below rummaged through books of cloth samples, or flipped through the photos of male models in *Gentleman's Quarterly*.

Like many urban streets in North America, College near Bathurst has radically been transformed. And not for the better. Granetstein's, the unique old house that served as a tailor shop next to my grandfather's, is gone, as is Stereo's Tavern. Mars Restaurant ("Food Out Of This World") has become a landmark, largely because of its superb bran muffins. The church on the corner of College and Bathurst, after it was no longer used as a church, was at first employed as a halfway house for patients from the Clarke Institute of Psychiatry. A few of the out-patients would hang around my grandfather's shop because my father and uncles always enjoyed "characters." Later, the church was gutted and turned into an upscale condominium. In a concession to the city's historic sites board, the developers preserved the steeple and stained glass window. They must wonder whether it was those holy vestiges that jinxed them. They were unable to sell even half the units and went bankrupt two years after the project was completed.

Today, between an uninspired, concrete condo-complex and a featureless, grey medical building, my grandfather's tailor shop squats, an unfashionable reminder. My grandfather passed away years ago but a large, framed black and white photo of him hangs

The Tailor Shop

above the triple-sided mirror. He is staring down at his three sons, keeping an eye on them. There isn't much to watch now that custom tailoring is all but dead. The last time I was in the shop my father sat at the large order desk playing solitaire.

My father still keeps cats and no longer cares whether they appear in the front of the store. I recently drove past Sherman Custom Tailors on my way to a restaurant further west in the Italian district. The shop was totally darkened. In the window I could barely make out a sign. On cardboard in my father's hand were large words in black magic-marker: CLOTH — HALF PRICE. And underneath, in equally large letters: FREE KITTENS, ASK INSIDE.

SILVER BRAIDS

I remember my grandmother, seated in our den, her head cradled in the palm of her hand. She is gently rocking back and forth, her thick black shoe rising and falling in rhythm to an Old World ballad playing on our stereo. She stares down at the carpet, lost either in reverie or blankness. I cannot say which, for my grandmother, by her own choosing, is mute. I have never heard her speak a word. Her profile, dark, angular, cavernous, bordered by silver hair plaited into tight braids, takes on the Semitic prominence one notes in the photographed faces of North American Indians.

There are times when my grandmother's braids create a different impression. They are more the hairstyle of a young girl than of a woman in her seventies, contributing to my perception of her as mad. That is how members of her own family have presented her. But to say that someone is insane or crazy is often a dismissal, covering an unwillingness to confront the suffering of the life, its tragedy and terror. The poet, Theodore Roethke, wrote: "What's madness but nobility of soul/At odds with circumstance?"

And what were the circumstances of my grandmother's life? It is impossible for me to discover all the essential details now that she is gone. At that late stage in her life when I was tempted to ask her questions, she had stopped talking. Nor have I been able to gather many promising anecdotes from my father, uncles and aunts. When I speak to them about her, they seem bewildered

Silver Braids

and fall silent. It is as if her life had created some tremendous void in them, which prohibits words. All I have been given is a biographical outline, one or two related details, and my own sparse memories.

What I know is that she was my grandfather's village sweetheart and that he, after working in Toronto for a few years, returned to his former home in Poland to marry her and bring her to Canada. My grandfather's return to a country he despised, the arduous journey back across the Atlantic and Europe, as well as my grandmother's leaving, at the tender age of sixteen, her parental home and family — all these facts testify to my grandparents' passion for one another. Yet in North America their relationship began to erode. As the years went by, they grew more and more apart, for as much as my grandfather embraced the New World, my grandmother retreated from it. While he wore fashionable pinstriped suits and took in the latest motion pictures, she stayed secluded in her house, making the occasional foray for food or clothing. She never encountered enough of the world beyond her self-imposed ghetto to learn even the most rudimentary English. They lived together until the end, but were in fact leading separate lives. My grandmother was too fearful to travel, so in their later years my grandfather flew to Miami Beach alone. I've heard rumours that he had a long-standing relationship with another woman.

My grandparent's troubled marriage was evoked in a comment made by my mother at my grandmother's funeral. My grandfather had been dead for two years; as my grandmother's coffin was lowered into the grave adjoining his, over which a large headstone would soon bear both their names, I heard my mother whisper: "Look. Even in death he can't get away from her." My mother's sarcasm was founded on something more than the universal conflict between women and their mothers-in-law. For a good many years my grandmother, reclusive, uncommunicative, had been considered a burden to her family, while my grandfather, up until his death, had been a provider. He still was, considering that the men's tailoring business he had built — now run by my father and uncles — continued to feed us.

If life had been difficult for my grandfather as an immigrant to Canada at the turn of the century, it had been nearly impossible for my grandmother. She had six children to deal with, one of them mentally retarded, as well as the memory of a baby she had inadvertently killed. If the Industrial Age gave us the model of the absent father — the shift worker, the travelling salesman, the struggling shopkeeper — it also gave us the archetype of the mad mother. In my grandmother, one sees the shadows of a multitude of women, estranged, burdened, lacking support.

An immigrant is asked to incorporate two diverse cultures, to dream in a new language. To achieve this, one must either leave the Old World behind or attempt, through an act of imagination and will, to amalgamate it with the new. But because it is impossible to completely do either, one is left with loose ends, feelings of alienation and incompleteness. And so one remains a D.P. — a displaced person, a double person.

My grandmother was one who could not even attempt the leap. She was plagued by homesickness, by a primal, tactile connection to the village where she had grown up. In the worn trunk she had brought with her from Poland, she preserved a world that was deeply irrational: a world of folklore and fear, of demons and dybbuks, of haunted loaves of bread and cats whose very glances were infectious. Everywhere there lurked the Evil Eye. You had to tie a red ribbon to a baby's cradle to ward off the Evil Eye. You had to spit three times after paying someone a compliment to ward off the Evil Eye. Once, convinced that an infant of hers had been touched by this destructive presence, she recalled an Old World remedy, filled a metal bucket with hot coals and passed it over the baby, muttering prayers and incantations. The white-hot coals burnt through the bottom of the bucket, spilling onto her infant son. He died a few days later from his severe burns.

She spent months in and out of a psychiatric hospital. Who can imagine those wards of the 1930s? She was given shock treatments. In her later years, the years I remember, what was she thinking or seeing as she sat in our den? Was her mind like a snowy terminal screen, a white electric void? She must have picked up the strains of those Yiddish songs coming from the stereo. There was a very old oval-framed photograph of a pious man in our basement. It was the oldest photograph our family possessed and it was of my grandmother's grandfather. My father referred to him as Zelig the Klezmer. Klezmer music is the folk music of East European Jews and my grandmother's grandfather had been a professional musician, fiddling and singing at weddings and festivals. But though my grandmother could hear music, and though music was in her blood, (in her youth she had displayed a beautiful singing voice), she could no longer produce it. She communicated with her daughter Doris, in whose house she lived until her death, through hand signals and moans. The doctors, when consulted, reported that she was in acceptable health for a woman her age, that there was nothing seriously wrong with her. As with all persons suffering from a psychosomatic disorder, her body had become a metaphor, a mysterious map of hidden sources of pain.

Her worst period came during the middle years of the 1930s when my father, her youngest, was a boy. She spent much of those years in the hospital, brought home some weekends, dazed, depressed. It is ironic that we refer to that historical period as the Great Depression. My grandfather, to support his family, had to do his tailoring long into the night. He had a cot brought to the store and slept there, going home only on weekends. Except for the care he received from his older sister, my father, a very young boy at the time, might have been considered an orphan.

When my grandmother died in the home of her daughter, I drove with my father to the house. My aunt, who had cared for my grandmother over the past decade, attending as best she could to her complaints, came to the vestibule and hugged my father and me.

"She's gone," she said. And then in a lower voice, as if to confirm it, she repeated, "She's gone."

Some of my uncles, aunts, and cousins were already gathered in the kitchen, whispering, weeping softly. I followed my father up the narrow staircase to my grandmother's room. I had never seen a dead person before and felt afraid. I did not know what emotions my father would express, nor did I know how I would respond.

When my father saw his mother he let out a loud, anguished cry which startled me. Then he lay down on the bed and held onto her, sobbing deeply and calling to her as if he could call her back from the dead. I felt embarrassed to be there, to witness my father's passion. I wanted to turn and walk back down the staircase but I was held by the image of my grandmother. Her head was tilted on the pillow, her cheeks drawn in, her nose narrowed, her mouth slightly open. She looked as if she had been frozen in the process of letting out her final breath. Her face, like the pillow, was chalky; it seemed as if she had sunk back into the bed, as if in death she had withdrawn one final, definitive step into the inanimate world. Most of all, I recall her white hair. It was loose, sprawling on the pillow. There was something liberating about that, as though she was finally free of those tight braids of the past. Yet I remember thinking, as my father continued to weep, that there was something not right about it, for that loose flowing hair did not represent my grandmother. It did not express the terrible tensions that had been her life.

VOID AND VOICE:
NOTES FROM POLAND

I. Two years ago I travelled to Poland. In a sense I was travelling backwards in both time and space, making the reverse trip my grandfather had made 85 years before when as a young teenager he left his small town and worked his way as a tailor across Europe. Travelling from country to country, it took him two years to save steerage. He sailed from England and arrived in Toronto in the winter of 1904. Unable at first to find work at his trade, he spent his first Canadian winter doing the most Canadian thing of all — shovelling snow. The sidewalks then were wooden: I can see horse buns steaming in the snow; I can hear the crew he worked with — a melange of foreign accents.

I, on the other hand, made the reverse trip in less than a day, was served food by attractive stewardesses, my travel expenses paid for by my government's arts council. All of that, plus the mere fact that I existed, that my parents were not part of an ash heap, points to the indisputable wisdom of my grandfather in leaving a continent for which he had nothing but contempt. "Europe is a sewer," he would say; then thinking of his new country, he would ruefully add, "...but who knows you here?"

I had received a grant to do research in the USSR on the Russian poet Osip Mandelstam, and it seemed to me a good opportunity to stop en route in Poland and visit the places my grandparents had come from. I had a wish to see with my own eyes where they had once lived and where those they had left behind had been murdered. A morbid wish? Difficult to say. A people's grave, especially if it is one's own people, is a very special place in one's psychic map. Yet what was this impulse to actually see it, having already watched so much film footage and read so many books on the subject? Wasn't that enough? People once made pilgrimages to sacred places; living in a century godless and violent, where we are suspicious of good but maintain a strong belief in the persistence of evil, the numinous for us has shifted from saint's shrines to scenes of destruction. Or perhaps we have a predisposition to the effects of loss. As for myself, I have always found ruins more moving than buildings that are intact. The Wailing Wall, for instance, would not be half as powerful a symbol if its other three walls were still standing.

Through chance and circumstance, I have travelled to many countries, more than I would have chosen since most are a disappointment. After a time, being a tourist becomes merely an exercise, an accumulating of numerous dates and sites. It can be difficult to maintain an imaginative connection to a foreign place and I have often had the uneasy realization that the book I was reading on the tour bus was more interesting than the tour, which is another way of saying that mind travel is usually superior to the geographical kind.

Yet Poland was a country that did not disappoint me, mainly because I had a mission and because there is a multitude of ghosts there. It is a Double Country, a land of two worlds — the living and the dead. In Warsaw, a cluster of grey apartment buildings sits on the site of the old Jewish ghetto, and near a park with swings is a red brick wall left from the war, pock-marked from mortar and bullets. A restaurant advertises "Jewish-style soup." A theatre group is producing a Yiddish comedy translated into Polish. The rebuilding that has gone on in Warsaw since the war, unlike that in German cities, has not been an attempt to expunge the past. In Poland, the past is always intruding into the present. We each carry within us our personal, racial and cultural histories. The point at which those pasts collide with our contemporary existence may serve as the point of illumination. For a poet, it is often the point of poetic tension. Since the poet is a sound engineer, one who mixes the voices of living with those of the dead, Poland, for me at least, served as a poetic catalyst.

Void and Voice: Notes from Poland

II. I had seen so much black and white footage of WW II that I was shocked to arrive in a sunny, bright Warsaw. The Warsaw of my mind would be grey, overcast, people scurrying furtively through twisted streets, in and out of narrow, dilapidated houses. An expressionist nightmare; a poor man's Caligari. The narrow streets were mostly gone, replaced by wide Stalinist avenues; where there had once been claustrophobic tenements rich in personality, there were now impersonal, homogeneous Soviet-style concrete hulls used for factories, hotels, office or apartment buildings, all indistinguishable from one another.

In the oldest part of the city they are painstakingly rebuilding Old Town from photographs, some extant blueprints and memory. It is a futile gesture. For the new lacks the patina that accumulates on the old and gives it flavour, and the small brightly coloured shops there remind one of the faked foreign country sections in Disney World. There is an organic geological aspect to cities, created by time and the erosion from soles and tires, that cannot be simulated.

One of the few green, shaded and beautiful spots in the city is an old Jewish cemetery on the border of what was once the ghetto. The tombstones are dark and brooding with their chiselled Hebrew hieroglyphs. Every cemetery has its own personality, oddly akin to the actual lives of its denizens. Take the graveyards of British soldiers you come across in Madras, or Khartoum, or Singapore. All the regimented crosses, as if those military souls were still marching. Or the small Presbyterian cemeteries in rural Ontario, with plenty of space between each modest stone as if breathing room were still a priority for those farmers and their wives. Here, by contrast, is a ghetto within what had once been a ghetto. The stones are so close they almost touch. They lean this way and that like crooked teeth. The density is both oppressive and stimulating. Oppressive because of the weight of so much stone, so much gravity, sadness and heaviness; stimulating because of the cultural anarchy here, the social mulch. Different centuries are next to one another as are different personalities: an administrator next to a musician; a mystical rabbi next to a rationalist philosopher; a young girl next to a prostitute. The odd juxtapositions that conjure for a moment the enormous diversity of that community.

Of course these are the more fortunate buried here, having died before the Catastrophe. Their presence reminds us of the greater absence just beyond the gate of this burial ground. For those who lived to suffer in the Warsaw ghetto are not buried here. Some are in mass, anonymous graves, lime-filled so as to prevent the spread of typhus; many others, like those young resistance fighters commemorated in a statue in this cemetery, are beneath the brick and asphalt of the hideous apartments you can see from the gate. Yet the vast majority of those half million inhabitants who were forced to survive in an area one and a quarter square miles and surrounded by a wall crowned with barbed wire and broken glass, are not buried anywhere. Treblinka is less than a two-hour car drive from here.

III. At the entrance to the Jewish cemetery is the statue of a bald, slender man in an overcoat. It is Janusz Korczak; he is walking, holding a small child whose arms are wrapped about his neck, her cheek pressed to his face. He is leading another child by the hand. Other children follow behind. A type of Peter Pan, I think, and cannot prevent myself from making a morbid joke about the Never-Never Land he is leading them to.

Korczak was a double-man living in a double-city. This is attested to firstly by the Polishness of his adopted name; he was born Henryk Goldszmit and was Jewish. He was a medical doctor, educator and author who ran a famous orphanage on Krochmalna Street. He wrote widely-read child psychology texts with titles like *The Child's Right to Respect*. His children's novel, *King Matt the First*, was as famous in Eastern Europe as *Peter Pan* in the Anglo-Saxon world. In a regular 15-minute programme on Polish radio he appeared as the Old Doctor, giving advice to those suffering from physical or psychological problems. Polish reaction to him was ambivalent. In 1936, anti-Semites forced him off the air, claiming a Jew should not shape the minds of Catholic children. In the following year, The Polish Academy of Literature awarded him the Golden Laurel for his literary achievements. This mixed reaction followed him to the train that would take him and his children to the death camp.

When the Germans began liquidating the ghetto and ordered

Void and Voice: Notes from Poland

his orphanage evacuated, Korszak led a procession of two hundred children to the waiting freight cars. Refusing last minute offers of help to escape from some Catholic admirers, he said, "You do not leave a sick child alone in the night." An eyewitness to the procession, one Nachum Remba, whose report was preserved in the secret archives of the ghetto, tells us: "All of the children had formed ranks in rows of four, with Korczak at their head, his eyes lifted to the sky; holding two children by their small hands... Even the police stood still and saluted. When the Germans saw Korczak, they asked, 'Who is this man?'"

Other eye-witnesses tell us that as the procession passed the Children's Hospital, heading toward Karmelicka Street, Poles could be heard shouting, "Goodbye, good riddance, Jews." All who witnessed the event report that Korczak maintained his composure.

The grass around Korczak's statue is overgrown, unkempt with large weeds, as if Polish reaction to him were still ambivalent. From where the statue is situated, you gaze out beyond the gates of the cemetery at the chipped, discoloured Warsaw tenements. A woman in a torn cotton dress hangs laundry near a rusted swing set. A patch of dried grass here and there. Two abandoned grey-brick buildings with shattered windows. The scene beyond the cemetery seems so sterile, so lifeless, that one feels with certainty that there is more going on within the gates, on those cracked and brooding headstones, than without.

IV. I did not want to like the Polish people. Though there were examples of heroism and altruism amongst them, in general their treatment of the Jews seemed to prohibit any liking. But the truth is I did like them. I found them hospitable, tenacious, at times intense and passionate, and indolent in a rebellious sort of way. I saw them as the Italians of Eastern Europe, though far more depressed and, perhaps, complex. Like the Italians, they were anarchists at heart. They despised their current masters — the Soviets — and were suspicious of their own leaders. It was a suspicion born out of the ravages of their own tragic history and struck me as an especially healthy attitude. Yet there was something disturbing and dangerous about them too. They drink too much and when they are drunk do not become joyous but temperamental and at times violent. My sense was that civilization sits uneasily with them, and that when released from it, there is anger at having been repressed and perhaps guilt at having been freed. In his book *Native Realm: A Search for Self-Definition,* the poet Czeslaw Milosz states that the Pole, "...wears a corset...After a certain amount of alcohol, it bursts open revealing a chaos that is not often met with in European countries." Milosz explains that this corset is a social one, that the Pole's problem is one of duty toward the collective (i.e. Church, nation, class). In his chapter entitled "Catholic Education," Milosz intuits that Poles are badly christened: "Religion is rarely an inner experience... most often it is a collection of taboos grounded in habit and tribal prejudices." Christian ethics then remain tied to social identifications; hence the Pole's shifting attitude toward the Jew, depending on whether he perceives him as part of his society or an outsider, the latter being the usual case.

Yet despite all of this, one realizes that the Poles could never have organized an annihilation like the one that was carried out. In the first place they are too anarchistic to organize on that scale and secondly, they could not sustain such evil over so long a period of time. One can imagine flare-ups, drunken murders, sporadic pogroms, but not railway networks, tattooing, bagging human ashes for use as fertilizer.

There was another factor that made it difficult for me to dislike the Poles. I had a tremendous admiration for their literature. At least their modern literature. I know nothing of their classical writings. But from the moment I read the poems of Zbignief Herbert, Milosz, Wat, the stories of Borowski, the novels of Konwicki, I felt I had encountered an important literature, one which spoke in a voice that contended honestly with the struggles of the human spirit in the wake of the annihilation.

One other factor. On an internal flight from Warsaw to Cracow I read an article in the Polish airline's *Lot* magazine about a family of seven who had been shot in their farmyard as punishment for hiding Jews. It is difficult, perhaps impossible, to judge those who were given a choice to act or to remain silent when to act could mean certain death. The Jews, as victims, were given no such choice: all were slated for death. In the ghetto however, a different choice was created: to die passively, under the illusion

Void and Voice: Notes from Poland

that there would be a moment of respite, or die fighting, fully aware of the enemy's intent, and therefore beyond illusion.

V. Museums are curious institutions. The word actually means "house of the muses" but no artist, to my knowledge, ever founded one. They are the creations of those with power and wealth. Man lives and creates; afterwards, someone places the manifestations in a house for future generations to ponder. What one feels in a museum is wonder mixed with the pleasure of the survivor for what one sees is most often dead. Not only are the animals and humans dead, but so are the species or, in the case of humans, the civilizations they belonged to: their crafts, weapons, costumes and jewellery, all in the realm of the dead while those viewing are in the realm of the living. Museums are civilization's mausoleums; perhaps they serve to assuage our collective guilt over those we have lived beyond, or alternately help us feel superior to them and confirm our belief in newness and progress. It must be noted that the first museum was founded at Alexandria, Egypt, by Ptolemy I, one of Alexander the Great's generals who seized Egypt in the late 300's B.C. One imagines he filled it with items from his conquest. It is also worth noting that his museum became a university.

The Museum of the Jewish People and their Artifacts in Warsaw is in an old house on three levels, small and poorly lit. The "artifact" section is on the main floor, but there are very few artifacts. Only a small number of enlarged photographs of Warsaw's great synagogues before the war. The exhibit on the second floor is much more interesting. A number of enlarged edicts and posters from the German Occupation, warning, threatening, prohibiting. There are anti-Semitic artifacts on display which were used by the SS: an ashtray in the shape of a pig with a man's feet jutting out of the mouth and the caricature of a Jew's head sticking out the pig's anus. There is the enlarged photo of a Polish peasant woman who was caught harbouring Jews, surrounded by SS with a sign on her chest that reads

I am the louse-loving bitch
Consider me dead

On the walls are grainy photographs of young resistance fighters — men and women who fought in the ghetto. And the dates of their brief lives. The eldest — Abraham Diamant (astonishingly the same name as my maternal grandfather), 1900-1943; and the youngest — Eliezer Blones, 1930-1943. And other photos: a man in flames leaping from a burning building; the haggard fighters, arms upraised, being marched out by the smiling (why are they always smiling?) German soldiers. But I go back to the photos of the ghetto fighters. Some of those faces could have been found in my high school graduation yearbook. This brings me closer to the event for had I been born a decade earlier, had my grandfathers not left Poland, I would most likely have been amongst those herded to the Umschlagplatz, the station which now bears the memorial names of a handful of the masses who were shipped out. Or — and I prefer to think of myself this way — I may have died throwing Molotov cocktails at the helmeted soldiers.

The museum is open for a few hours each morning. I am the only one in attendance. The entire time I am there a tape is playing; I am struck by one particular song — a female voice singing in Yiddish. My knowledge of Yiddish is very sparse, but a woman whom I will meet on my way out who helps administer the museum explains to me that it is a song that a Partisan of the ghetto wrote a short time before its destruction. In it, a woman addresses her infant:

> *Child, if you survive*
> *O, if you survive*
> *You will only understand the meaning of this*
> *When you listen to the silence.*

VI.   On the day I plan to visit Auschwitz, something in me resists going. Even the phrase "visit Auschwitz" seems to me absurd, as if it were like visiting a friend. A better term might be "experience" or "contend with." To stand at the place of great evil.

An extremely hot June day. After making my way to the railroad station in Cracow, I am told I had been given the wrong

Void and Voice: Notes from Poland

information about train departures at my hotel. The next train to Oswiecim (the Polish name for Auschwitz) is not until 1:30 — a three-hour wait. I use this information as an excuse to leave, telling myself it was not meant for me to go.

But as I leave the station, a taxi driver approaches and asks if I would like to go to Auschwitz. "Two hours there and then, if you wish, down the road to Birkenau." The man speaks fairly good English (I discover later that he lived for two years in Philadelphia). He is short, dark-skinned, soft-spoken, and carries a genuine air of solemnity befitting a ferryman into the land of ghosts. At that moment I see him as my appointed intermediary, sent to ensure my getting to Auschwitz. How had he known that that was where I was planning to go, or is Auschwitz the only place a tourist would go by train from Cracow? In any event, his intervention gives the entire day a sense of destiny. For the next three days, this taxi driver whose name is Kazimier Olesiak, or Kaz as he likes to be called, drives me to all the places I wish to see, acting as an intelligent and sensitive guide and translator. From the start he seems to be aware of the seriousness of my visit; most probably he has served this role as Charon before.

Once we pass the enormous steel mills and factories on the outskirts of Cracow, we enter farm country, field after field of what Kaz calls "yellow carpets"— acres of flax. Gentle sloping hills, spotted cows, blue sky. Did the victims see, through the cracks in the boxcars, these colours of a children's primer on their way to the camps? I know that it would have been more appropriate to travel this route by train but I am glad I didn't; being in a car distances me somewhat from the experience and allows me to bear my confrontation with history.

VII.   Before touring Auschwitz you enter an auditorium to view a film. The day I am there, the hall is filled almost entirely with Polish schoolchildren; aside from them and me, there is a contingent of about 25 East Germans. The film we are shown is less graphic than most I have seen, perhaps because many of the visitors here are children. I am surprised by the lack of any mention of Jews in the film, an omission that is continued throughout Auschwitz. The Poles have treated Auschwitz as primarily a Polish tragedy, which in part it was; and the schoolchildren are there to have their nationalist sentiments bolstered. But by not emphasizing the fact that Jews were the primary target, official Poland makes obvious its anti-Semitic policy.

Each country that lost people has been given a barrack to convert into a sort of pavilion honouring the dead, with photos, mementos, testimonials. There is one for Italy, one for France, for Russia. But none has been given to Israel, which would be the country to represent Jews. The official reason given is that Poland does not have diplomatic relations with Israel. But such official reasons rarely fool people.

As I walk through the barracks turned pavilions, I have two responses: one, that I am sickened by the thought of what occurred here; the other, however, is disrespectful — namely, that I am in a theme park. And what is the theme? Inhumanity, Death, Evil? To the credit of the Poles they have not, like the Germans, prettified or overly cleaned up the camps. Still, any sort of organizing has the effect of a hand coming afterward to mitigate the rawness of the original horror. The prosthetic limbs, shoes, toothbrushes, combs, eyeglasses, women's hair, must have been ghastly to come upon by the liberators; but labelled in display bins behind glass, their shock value is reduced. I fear this is another museum, another safe tribute to the dead. Or perhaps I have seen so many photographs of these objects that I am immune to their sadness. This is the most discomforting thought of all, that this place has become a cliché of itself.

Yet if I do not find the horror I expected, I find unexpected, ghastly ironies. In the display of luggage where each suitcase carries the name of its owner and place of origin, I pick out the following three: a Marie Kafka, Prague; an M. Frank, Amsterdam; a J. Freud, Vienna. Which reminds me that it wasn't only humans that were swallowed here, but an entire culture whose particular dynamism was largely the result of its relationship with the gentile world that surrounded it. "Without the Jews it would be boring," many Polish intellectuals, even those anti-Semitic, claimed before the war. Is Europe a less vital place now that it has rid itself of its Jews, its Kafkas, Franks, and Freuds?

Those suitcases and those names — was that an ironic joke played by some cultured curator here? Or prophecy. Later in the day, as I enter the gas chamber and crematorium, I will note the

Void and Voice: Notes from Poland

initials K.S. scratched over the chamber entrance and wonder at my believing the day is my day, the visit, my visit, as if the historical muse had been anticipating me. Which is perhaps a projection of the necessary egocentricity every author momentarily possesses, believing he or she alone has been chosen.

VIII. I see something else at Auschwitz that impresses me. It is a map that was found on an SS officer who worked here. The map is of Europe and it is exceptional because Oswiecim, which is really a small town, is depicted as gigantic, a major centre, while Rhodes, Riga, Minsk, Paris, and Amsterdam have been reduced to pinpoints. The map is saying that the hub of the new world order is Auschwitz; that is the new capital and all roads lead there. Or another way of perceiving it is Auschwitz as a huge mouth swallowing the world. Ultimately it is not a true geographical map but rather a picture of a state of mind.

Yet not only the perpetrators, but the prisoners too saw Auschwitz as a world. Or an inverted, ironic version of the world. Geographical place names were given to areas and peoples in the camp. "Canada" was the area where goods taken from those about to be gassed were stored, since in those prisoners' minds Canada was, perhaps rightly, associated with riches; "Mexico" referred to the poor, hastily built barracks where 15,000 Hungarian women were housed in intolerable conditions. A "Muslim" was one who appeared sick, weak, depressed and near death. Irony is a way of coping with the harshness or absurdity of the real. It is also a form of rebellion through language.

In Auschwitz, the real was the business of death, or, death as a business. Firstly, only those prisoners deemed fit enough to work escaped the initial selection. In the ultimate exploitation, those prisoners were fed next to nothing and worked until they dropped dead. They were disposable work units. Whether killed immediately or after months of gruelling labour, their bodies were used for commercial purposes: fertilizer, soap, hair woven into material, etc. Those companies which bid on contracts to build the camps and supply the gas were not shady fly-by-nighters, but most often large, reputable German firms.

With the Industrial Revolution, man saw his fellow man as a machine, capable of working long hours with little pay. It would be a diminishment of the enormity of Auschwitz to say this was the prime motivation behind its inhumanity. There is something far more feral about the sadism and cruelty that was acted out. Yet just as the geographical place names prisoners gave it linked it to the real world, so too did its business logic. It is fair to say that the depersonalization and dehumanization inherent in the modern industrial society was carried to its ultimate there. Whether that in itself provides a criticism of our society or whether it simply means that anything taken to extremes can produce such evil is for the reader to decide.

IX. A few years ago, at a Conference for Teachers of the Holocaust, I heard a survivor, the novelist Arnost Lustig, talk about his experience in Auschwitz. He reported that one day he was standing by the wire fence, when suddenly, in the women's camp, he saw a long line of running, naked female figures. They were being hurried along by the male guards cracking whips. Lustig had been separated from his mother upon arrival at the camp; not hearing from her or of her since then, he assumed she was dead. He told us that watching those naked women running under the whips made him feel glad she had perished. It was a long line of women. To his horror he saw that the last face, the very last face in the line, was indeed that of his mother. She had survived to suffer this.

Lustig told a number of stories illustrating situations where there was no acceptable ethical response. The point he wished to make was that absolutely nothing he had learned as a student, from the teachings of Moses, Jesus, Buddha, or from those of Plato and Socrates, could in any way help him with the daily dilemmas of survival in the camp. It was as if he had to invent a new self each day to live out that day. If none of the great teachers of civilization could help him there, the question arises: was Auschwitz a product of our civilization or antithetical to it? Or both?

X. One kilometre down the road from Auschwitz is Birkenau. Here is the infamous railroad entrance I have seen in so many films and photographs, and the endless lines of barracks that stretch without end. Auschwitz had the feeling of being enclosed,

Void and Voice: Notes from Poland

contained, while this place seems infinite.

I am the only visitor. The schoolchildren are not brought here it seems, nor are the German tourists. I can understand why. This is not a theme park. There are no exhibits or pavilions here. Not a thing has been touched since the war ended. Weeds, broken barracks, and the shattered stacks of the crematoria. Here the ghosts thrive, unlike at Auschwitz where they are crowded out by so many tourists and displays. Even if you don't see the ghosts you can sense them in the unbroken silence of this place. For if Auschwitz is a world, with geographical names, this place is cosmic, posing questions which are metaphysical.

A ghost is really an absence that reminds us of a presence — a lost presence. It is an absence that draws us in and asks us to speak for it. Withdrawal is an important theme in Jewish religious thought. The prophet Isaiah cries out in anguish, "Truly Thou art a God Who hides Himself" while the later Cabbalists theorize that God's withdrawal from the world leaves a void which asks to be filled through creation. A voice to fill the void. Poetry as it relates to loss.

But what sort of voice can fill this void, I wonder, staring at the ruins of this camp which seem to go on and on. Is silence the appropriate response to this great silence, as some have suggested? I do not believe so. Yet the problem of how to find the appropriate tone to respond to this silence is a difficult one. For this is neither the silence of a living forest nor that of a cemetery.

And I wonder too whether there is such a thing as true silence, for a human being that is. Perhaps when we speak of silence we are only distinguishing between inward and outward speaking. There is a prayer one finds in Kierkegaard's journal: "Father in Heaven, it is indeed only the moment of silence in the inwardness of speaking with one another." For who standing here could not be speaking with himself? Or with the ghosts who have their own underground language?

XI. The night after my visit to Auschwitz, I lie in my hotel room reading. In the room next to mine two couples, very drunk, are arguing. I have never encountered as many drunken people as here in Poland. I find this unsettling. There is something unknown and potentially explosive about a drunk. Most drink after dark, but many can also be seen stumbling through the streets all hours of the day where they carry on self-chastening monologues; they occasionally shake a fist or wave a hand in resigned disgust at a passer-by. This is the dark, dismal, self-hating side of the Polish soul.

Those few Polish Jews who survived the Shoah (a term preferable to Holocaust since it is Hebrew and means annihilation) and did not immigrate, returned to their towns and villages, many to be murdered, incredibly, in pogroms *after* the war.

As recently as 1984, the Polish government, to help fend off criticism of itself, was able to actively promote Jew-hatred — in a nation where there were virtually no Jews left. The curious phenomenon of Jew-hatred in countries where there are only phantoms: in Austria, Poland, the Ukraine. The Jew as an idea, a mythological being, a projection. Representing what? The greedy capitalist? The zealous communist? The Christ-killer? The Christ-denier?

Although this anti-Semitic campaign had been going on for months, the *Toronto Star* chose to headline the story on its front page on December 23 of that year, one day before Christmas Eve. Given the history of Jewish/Christian relations, I couldn't help but wonder at the timing.

I believe it was George Steiner who said that a person does not really know what it means to be a Jew until he or she is the parent of a Jew. Every Jewish parent who looks at photos of the children in the Warsaw ghetto sees the faces of his or her own children. This is what is meant by *living history.* The *Star's* account of renewed anti-Semitism in Poland and its timing, produced an unease in me that resulted in the following poem, which I wrote the next night, Christmas Eve. It is entitled, simply, "December 24."

> *Silent night, our furnace whirrs.*
> *On my way to bed I stop*
> *outside my daughter's door,*
> *her breath*
> *the rhythm of a small sea.*

Void and Voice: Notes from Poland

Outside, stars
burn like splinters of ice,
smoke out of chimneys
coils through the mute
and endless dark

I will wait another moment
listening
for my daughter's breath
before I turn out the light.

I am glad that I chose an indirect and as it happened, universal way to express the dis-ease I was feeling those cold December days. It can speak to many people. The words *furnace, chimneys, smoke, mute,* and the phrase *endless dark,* all arise naturally in the poem — nothing is forced — but for me each of those words possesses a second significance. *Silent night* carries for me a special irony, and between each line I can hear the whispers of the phantom children.

XII.   The book I was reading as I lay in my hotel room was Primo Levi's haunting novel, *If Not Now, When,* the story of Jewish partisans fighting in the countryside of WW II Poland.

My trip to Poland, had, so far, a prophetic air to it, from the recognition of the photos of the partisan fighters in Warsaw to my initials scratched over the chamber door. I had in fact seen my double, who exists in time past. He is the one *who might have been here.* Borges, in his *The Book of Imaginary Beings,* tells us that to meet one's double, in most cultures, is ominous; however, "To the Jews the appearance of one's double was not an omen of imminent death. On the contrary, it was proof of having attained prophetic powers."

Prophecy — travelling backwards to dream forward. As I was falling off to sleep, I read those pages in Levi's book which describe a partisan raid against German soldiers on the outskirts of the Polish town of Chmielnik. Of all the thousands of small Polish towns, to mention the one I had planned to visit the next morning, the town of my maternal grandfather, seemed astonishing. An example of Jung's synchronicity, a term which always conjures for me the image of two clocks running into one another: time from the past colliding with time that is or will be. It seemed I was still being led, that some revelation was at hand.

XIII.   Chmielnik is north of Cracow and south of Kielce. Before the war it had a large Jewish community of some 12,000. When you enter the town you are in its central square: on one side is a park and garden; on the other a church; the other sides are lined with shuttered shops. In the doorways, women with scarves, silver-capped teeth.

Inside the church, darkness, broken by splashes of silver, red velvet, a mass of lit, finger-thin candles. There must be a grade school in the back or basement because before entering I see children playing outside and a young priest in a black cassock shouting after them.

There is a portrait of Jesus here, with blond hair and blue eyes. I have always been struck by how Jesus takes on the physical characteristics of the people amongst whom he is residing. In a small Italian church he resembles a Sicilian labourer; in a church in Mexico he has the dark, passionate eyes of Zapata. But seeing him here with Slavic features and upturned, blue beseeching eyes, makes me feel there is something not right. He seems so cut off from his Semitic roots, just as the people are cut off from theirs. He is a Jesus removed from the complexities of history, divorced from his origins; he has the face of a simple-minded nationalist, with no heaviness in his eyes.

There are books and books filled with testimony, speculation, socio-political factors, and economic-historical ones attempting to explain the reasons for anti-Semitism. But I am not standing in this ghost town for any explanations. Rather, an image: the Slavic face of Jesus the Jew. Considering what was done to His own people in that very square upon which His church stands, one wonders at the arrogance that could commandeer such an appropriation.

While I am in the church, Kaz is able to locate one of the town elders. He is wearing a navy blue cap, poorly-fitted jacket and pants. He tells us about the history of the town. I ask if he remembers the Diamond family, my mother's maiden name. Yes: he points to the place they lived: an apartment on top of a corner

Void and Voice: Notes from Poland

shop. I ask if he was here during the war. Yes; he tells me the Germans strictly divided the town between Poles and Jews. The Jews were not free to move. I ask him what happened to the Jews and he tells me it was not his business to know. He is not being mean. He is an old man with rotten teeth wondering what bad luck on this hot June day has brought this better-dressed foreigner to awaken sleeping phantoms. I ask him again and he tells me that a number were shot in the town; the rest were placed on trains to the camps.

Around the corner from the square is the synagogue. It is much larger than I expected. In that pre-war community of 12,000 there were few disbelievers.

The building has not been touched since the day the war ended. Its windows are boarded; some weeds grow from its grey brick. It sits there, frozen in time. Its very inertness makes it so imposing.

The old man explains the town is waiting to save the funds to renovate the synagogue. I ask what they are going to turn it into: apartments, factory, warehouse? No, you misunderstand, he says. What they wish to do is restore it to its original splendour.

I know that this is not true. Yet it is incredible to me that they have not torn the building down. The town is actually expanding, the population slightly larger than before the war. Except there is no one here who would make use of its synagogue. Perhaps they have left the synagogue standing because they are superstitious and do not wish to disturb or enrage the ghosts. What is superstition? A backward glance of guilt and shame? Again, the Poles' ambivalence toward the Jew, whether living or dead.

Behind the synagogue is the smaller building which once served as the school. Children would have played outside there. A scene like I just saw at the church except the black-garbed shouter would have been a rabbi rather than a priest. Now the Jewish school is used as a day-care.

The old man leads me to the Jewish cemetery on top of a small hill behind the synagogue. There is a sign: *No dumping of refuse. This is holy ground.* Without the sign no one would think this is a cemetery. It is a green open field; there is one solitary tombstone leaning at a 45-degree angle. I ask why there are no other tombstones: the old man is candid and tells me that over the years the stones were taken by the townsfolk for building purposes. I look down from the hill at the small post-war houses and wonder what verandah has my ancestor's name on it, face down towards the dark. I wonder too why they have left just one stone. To remind themselves that this is a cemetery? To make themselves feel that they are not completely immoral?

XIV. I am twelve or thirteen, sitting one evening in our den. A documentary begins on the television: the piled bodies, the gaping oven doors — images that always divide a life into a before and after. I recall my mother nervously wondering if maybe I shouldn't watch it and my father countering why not? As he put it, I should *know* what happened.

Shocking images. Yet there is something second-hand about film footage, whereas that squat ghostly building baking in the June heat was a rough confirmation I could run my hand along — literally, a touchstone. Mandelstam, the poet whose Petersburg I would be travelling to after this, also had an interest in buildings. His first book was titled *Stone*. Staring at the awesome structure of Notre Dame cathedral, he predicted that he too would "produce beauty from cruel weight." That was early in his career, early in the century, before Stalin's secret police, and the poet was referring to the weight of tradition, structure. Later on, persecuted by the regime, he would have revised it to the "cruel weight" of history and totalitarianism. Out of that he too would produce great poems. Though he was a Russian poet raised in Petersbourg, Mandelstam had been born in Warsaw. It is an irony of 20th century history that had his family never moved, his fate in one sense would have been tragically similar for he also perished in a camp (the only difference being it was one of Stalin's rather than Hitler's).

XV. I conclude with a footnote. Upon my return to Canada, I published a poem based on my visit to the Chmielnik cemetery, posing the same question I pose above: Why had the populace left one headstone standing? It seems the uncanniness of my entire adventure had followed me home, for the son-in-law of a former resident of Chmielnik who read my poem telephoned to say that he had the answer to the mystery of the single stone. He

Void and Voice: Notes from Poland

told me that his father-in-law had survived the war and returned to the town afterwards searching for fellow survivors. He found the cemetery completely desecrated; those stones not taken had been smashed to pieces. To counteract the void, he had a new stone placed at the grave of his father. In 1981 he returned and found it gone and had another put up.

I can report that in 1988 it was still there.

THE MASTER OF REPETITION

I first visited Jerusalem in the summer of 1969. I was residing in a youth hostel that served as a student dormitory during the school year. Each morning I would set out to discover a different section of the patchwork city: the Armenian Quarter, the Christian, the Jewish, the Muslim.

Jerusalem: no other city embodies such a powerful vision within the very syllables of its name. The promise of peace and brotherhood; a day when we will surrender our petty resentments, our hostilities. On that day we will accept and embrace one another. This dream of Jerusalem has proven to be unattainable, yet we refuse to relinquish it. That is why poets persist in reminding us that Jerusalem "breaks men's hearts."

There was a small diner where I used to eat in the old city, not far from the Damascus Gate. It served excellent lamb and the owner did not mind if I sat there after I had eaten, reading or watching. There was a spot across the narrow street that belonged to a blind beggar. He sat on a wooden crate all day long, like a sentinel at his post. I became fascinated with him and contrived to eat once a day at the diner so I could observe him.

He wore a wheat-coloured shirt and pants, and a tattered vest. His skin was quite dark. I did not know enough about the Middle East to ascertain whether he was an Arab or a Sephardic Jew from North Africa. The truth is, I did not want to find out; it seemed important to me to preserve the ambiguity of his origin.

The Master of Repetition

It was mostly tourists who gave him money. I suppose he had become invisible to those who lived or worked in the area; they took no notice of him. When someone dropped a coin into his palm he would run it deftly through his fingers, like a magician, to determine its value. Then he would smile and in a gesture of gratitude, raise the coin in a closed hand to his forehead and bow gently from the waist. Then he would slip the coin into a pouch.

I remember the first time I approached him. His eyelids were mostly closed but in the small space that was open I could see his eyes swimming helplessly. The rest of his face and his body were, as athletes say, quiet. I never once heard him utter a word and did not know if his silence was a sign of defiance or passivity. Perhaps he was mute. I eventually understood his silence to be a sign of his resoluteness, of his determination to wait.

Something about his spirit appealed to me and I never left the street without giving him money. I was tempted to try and speak to him with my limited Hebrew or to say a few words in Arabic; but this temptation always succumbed to the fear that I might disrupt the silent ritual of his giving thanks. The smile that he offered in return for coins was warm and generous; it seemed to radiate from the centre of his being. I was inclined to take this personally, as if the smile were meant for me. Once I gave him less than I usually did and immediately felt a pang of guilt; but his reaction was no different than usual and I was relieved. Once, in an overly generous mood, I gave him a larger sum. I was disappointed that his reaction was not more exuberant, that he was not more thankful. In fact, what amazed me about the beggar was that his reaction to all people and their almsgiving was identical, regardless of the amount they gave or whether they spoke to their cohorts in English, Dutch, German, or Japanese.

There was a repetitiveness to his life that I began to understand was religious. I tried to imagine myself seated in the same place, day after day, month after month, year after year. Interaction with those around me would be minimal. I would know all the scents from the nearby stalls and diners, as well as the foreign colognes of the tourists; I would know the types of shoes people wore from the sounds they made on the cobblestones.

And I used the sameness, the minimal routine of his life, to question life in general. After all, how much variety is there really in one's days, one's job, even in one's imagination? Rushing here and there, we attempt to mask the repetitiveness of existence. I thought of the most striking areas of Jerusalem I had visited. Mea-She'arim, where the ultra-orthodox Jews live, is like a centuries old Polish *shtetl*: the women in scarves and long skirts; the young men in caftans and white stockings, their side curls dangling from under ascetic, black hats. At first Mea-She'arim had seemed so unusual to me; but wasn't it, in fact, a replica of what had existed in the past, a mere repetition of history? The Arab Market, at first, was equally as exotic: dark labyrinthine streets, the succession of nameless stalls. But the stalls, I soon realized, were grouped together, offering the same merchandise. The pyramid of sheep heads in one butcher's stall was identical to that in another. And there seemed to be a myriad of leather handbags with the same embossed view of the Old City; several rugs depicting the Church of the Holy Sepulchre; many small, wooden camels.

    The blind beggar had fully accepted the repetitiveness of existence. There were only so many denominations of coins he would ever receive, only so many tones of voices he would hear from the passers-by. He would be neither richer nor poorer if he moved to another street to do his begging. I came to believe that this thin man, sitting on a wooden crate, embodied the vision of Jerusalem. His silence and patience stood for all who wait for the day of peace. His thankfulness, manifested in the fullness of his smile, made brothers and sisters of all who stopped for a moment from their hurrying, to give.

II

PRIMO LEVI AND THE UNLISTENED-TO STORY

Uncomfortable truths travel with difficulty.

— from *The Drowned And The Saved*

Some writers bequeath us unsettling questions. Such a writer was Primo Levi. A rationalist and craftsman, he avoided the pious, religious rhetoric that limits the work of some Holocaust authors, and the stylistic extremism that discredits others. His was a scientifically trained mind marked by acute powers of observation. This allowed him to serve as a trusted guide through the haze and smoke on our descent into the inferno, and if that image conjures Dante then all the better for Levi was no ordinary scientist but one gifted with an extraordinary literary sensibility. He was not only a memoirist and historian of the Holocaust, but possibly its finest artist. In addition, he had what few writers today possess — something important to say about human nature. If Levi was correct in proclaiming that the Lager provided him with a laboratory to understand that nature, then we now know that he himself was part of the experiment, for in the end, his collision with our century's most vast, cruel and pre-meditated crime left us not only with a host of insightful books, but also with a disheartening mystery — the suicide of their author. In her memoir, *Hope Against Hope*, Nadezda Mandelstam tells us: "The death of an artist is never a random event, but a last act of creation that seems to illuminate the whole of his life." She was speaking of her husband, Osip Mandelstam, whose death (he perished in the *gulag*; his crime — writing a poem critical of Stalin) revealed the intricate links between his life, his poetry, and what he referred to as "the wolfhound age." But in the case of a suicide one wonders if Mandelstam's word *illuminate* can apply. Speaking of the suicide of the philosopher and fellow Auschwitz survivor, Jean Améry, Levi says that it, "like other suicides admits of a cloud of explanations." On suicide and the absurd, Camus writes: "What sets off the crisis is almost always unverifiable." Levi, the scientist, would approve that last word. He would not sanction explanations, but he would endorse the probing, discussions and ruminations suicide invites.

If it is true that a writer's death is never a random event, then a self-inflicted death, the least random of all, will raise the stakes and increase the urgency with which we re-read his work. For re-read it we must. Our taboos against suicide are strongly imbedded, and the act itself implores us to go back and examine the victim's life, motives, perplexities. If the subject happens to be a writer, we feel compelled to return to his words in a search for clues we must have missed.

In the case of Primo Levi, this search takes on a unique urgency. The logic that leads to suicide is seldom rational and that is the reason why intellectuals were so shocked to hear of the death of this writer who had sided with the guardians of the Enlightenment, who had been unwilling to give himself over to subjectivity, either in the form of extreme passion or self-pity.

One of the more striking attempts to re-read Levi is Cynthia Ozick's "Primo Levi's Suicide Note," an essay which discusses the significance of his last book, *The Drowned And The Saved*. Put briefly, Ozick's thesis is that Primo Levi, in his writing, had presented himself as a fair-minded, just and detached scribe of the Holocaust, a man who despite his suffering, was without rancor, hatred, or the inclination to blame. She shares this perception with many other readers. Ozick compares Levi to "a vessel of clear water standing serenely apart." But according to her, there was something inauthentic in this, since Levi was repressing his deepest emotion — rage. While writing his final book, Levi ignites this emotion and expresses his animosity toward the German people; however, tortured by his own resentments, he feels compelled to turn the knife inward.

Hatred of the other, transformed into self-destruction, is basically a Freudian rendering of the cause of suicide and, in some instances, provides us with a reasonable explanation of an event we must ultimately regard as a mystery. Yet this theory implies a radical shift in the persona of Primo Levi. Ozick's implication that, in these pages, Levi tears off the mask of the polite, reticent and repressed analyst of the Holocaust and points a prophetic finger at his tormentors is not borne out by the book itself. It is too melodramatic an image to attach to Levi and one has the sense that Ozick, the novelist, has fictionalized her subject. The book refuses to be what she would have it — "a surrender to fury.... a biblical ululation." In fact, one of the more interesting chapters is entitled "The Gray Zone" which deals with the blurred morality that infected the prisoners and their superiors. Like Levi's other books, this one reveals ambiguities, attempts at truths rather than certainties. Yet it is also true that this final book is different from the others, though its difference is not its author's rage; rather, it is his frustration, his alienation, his doubts about transcendence. It is not, as Ozick believes, Levi's "most remarkable" book; in many ways it is his least imaginative, certainly his least literary. The book does not contain those unforgettable vignettes which lead to epiphany that are a trademark of Levi's finest writing, nor does it contain those characterizations that seem preserved in a timelessness reminiscent of classic folk tales. Throughout the book he chooses to explain rather than to reveal, as if the storyteller in him had given way to the polemicist, as if his belief in art had somehow withered.

I have never read Primo Levi as others have, as "a pure spirit", nor do I perceive an "absence of hatred" in his writing. This stereotyping of Levi has been an attempt to de-claw him as an author, and Ozick is correct when she states that his readers may be left with "a curious peacefulness." But the reasons for this have more to do with Levi's style, which elicits a feeling of transcendence in the reader, rather than with any avoidance of anger on his part. For Ozick is surely wrong when she claims that Levi's voice "has been consummately free of rage, resentment, violent feeling, or any overt drive to 'trade blows'." She is also inaccurate in leading us to believe that it is in this final book that Levi chooses the word "German" for his tormentors rather than "Nazi." Levi's scorn for the Germans is evident in the opening chapter of his first book, *Survival In Auschwitz:*

> This is the reason why three-year old Emilia died: the historical necessity of killing the children of Jews was self-demonstrative to the Germans... her parents had succeeded in washing her during the journey in the packed car in a tub with tepid water which the degenerate German engineer had allowed them to draw from the engine that was dragging us all to death.

If Levi's resentments are not obvious in these lines, then the reader has only to turn to the following paragraph in a later chapter from the same book. Levi is describing the grotesque activities of the Germans, given their knowledge that the war is coming to an end:

> But the Germans are deaf and blind, enclosed in an armour of obstinacy and of willful ignorance ... They construct shelters and trenches, they repair the damage, they build, they fight, they command, they organize and they kill. What else could they do? They are Germans. This way of behaviour is not meditated and deliberate, but follows from their nature and the destiny they have chosen.

In fact, in every book dealing with the Holocaust, Levi, without hesitation, points his finger at those responsible. In *Moments of Reprieve*, he writes a letter to a German chemist:

> I told him that if Hitler had risen to power, devastated Europe

Primo Levi and The Unlistened-to-Story

and brought Germany to ruin, it was because many good German citizens had behaved the way he did, trying not to see and keeping silent about what they did see.

If, from the beginning, Primo Levi did express his resentments, then we must ask what else was at the source of his anguish. A sort of answer will be found since it is my belief that this author, who strove for precision and honesty, fulfilled his obligation to himself, his fellow inmates and, most of all, his readers, by describing for us the nature of his deepest despair.

When I first read *Survival In Auschwitz*, I was struck most forcefully by the chapter "Our Nights," for there Levi relates the recurrent dreams of prisoners. The reader expects the first one — dreams of food:

> You not only see the food ... you are aware of its rich and striking smell; someone in the dream even holds it up to your lips, but every time a different circumstance intervenes to prevent the consummation of the act.

The other "collective dream" is unexpected. Levi pictures himself at home, after liberation, surrounded by relatives and friends. There is intense physical pleasure in the warmth of familiarity. He is relating his atrocious experiences:

> ...but I cannot help noticing that my listeners do not follow me. In fact they are completely indifferent: they speak confusedly of other things among themselves, as if I was not there... My dream stands in front of me, still warm, and although awake, I am still full of its anguish ... it is not a haphazard dream ... I have dreamed it not once but many times since I arrived here ... I have recounted it to Alberto and he confided to me, to my amazement, that it is also his dream and the dream of many others, perhaps of everyone. Why does it happen? Why is the pain of every day translated so constantly into our dreams, in the ever-repeated scene of the unlistened-to story?

For the reader, food dreams make sense since food is what the camp denies and it is essential to existence. But in what way is an "unlistened-to story" essential? In what way is it tied to survival? Levi himself provides us with an answer. In the midst of this dream he tells us:

> A desolating grief is now born in me, like certain barely remembered pains of one's early infancy. It is pain in its pure state, not tempered by a sense of reality ... a pain like that which makes children cry.

Communication is, in fact, a primal need; the infant's cries bring food, warmth and comfort; its smiles are met with approval; its frowns, with concern and anxiety. It is that asked-for help that Levi reminds us was humanly expected, yet totally lacking in the Lager.

My thesis is that at the heart of Levi's despair, and that of other survivor/writers like Améry, Celan, Borowski, is the unlistened-to story in its many different versions and guises. Levi has left us enough clues to know how much the ability to communicate with his fellow man meant to him. His epigraph to perhaps his finest literary achievement, *The Periodic Table*, is the Yiddish proverb: "Troubles overcome are good to tell," which he repeats in the body of his last book, *The Drowned and the Saved*. If the book is, as Ozick has shrewdly noted, a suicide note, then the note begins with precisely this concern, except that the unlistened-to story has become social, political and contemporary. Levi tells us that the first reports of the Nazi annihilation camps "delineated a massacre of such vast proportions, of such extreme cruelty and such intricate motivation that the public was inclined to reject them because of their very enormity." He goes on to quote SS militiamen who enjoyed admonishing their prisoners:

> "And even if some proof should remain and some of you survive, people will say that the events you describeare too monstrous to be believed: they will say that they are the exaggerations of Allied propaganda and will believe us, who will deny everything, and not you. We will be the ones to dictate the history of the Lagers."

Primo Levi and The Unlistened-to-Story

Even in the camps, the SS predicted the David Irvings, Ernst Zundels and the host of historical revisionists; even in the camps, the SS understood mankind's incapacity or unwillingness to believe. Levi then takes us back to his first book: "Strangely enough, this same thought ('even if we were to tell it, we would not be believed') arose in the form of nocturnal dreams produced by the prisoners' despair," and continues: "This is the theme to which we shall return ... how both parties, victims and oppressors, had a keen awareness of the enormity and therefore the noncredibilty of what took place in the Lagers..."

What informs his last book is not so much rage as frustration and futility, a suspicion that one is speaking into the wind. The background for this book were the atrocities in Cambodia, Viet Nam, South Africa, Central America; the real possibility of nuclear war; the rise of neo-fascism throughout Europe; the older generation denying the Holocaust and the younger generation indifferent to whether it occurred or not. The book's foreground is the Lager itself, not that which was contained within barbed wire, but what David Rousset termed "l'Univers Concentrationnaire," that entire world that built and fed off the camps — industrial companies, factories, farm combines, and such well known names as I.G. Farben, Siemens, Bayer. But Levi stretches this universe even further. He states that the lessons he learned in the Lager can be applied on a smaller scale to "what takes place in a big industrial factory." He links both the blind obedience that he witnessed in the Lager and the unfair system of privilege to "corporate mentality" and "corporate solidarity." It is as if the shadow of Auschwitz had seeped out to touch the technocratic, industrialized world, and that the line demarcating the camps and society had become part of what he terms "the gray zone." Levi warns that conditions may once more collide to produce an atrocity not unlike the one he experienced, and he asks us to be vigilant, "to sharpen our senses, distrust the prophets, the enchanters." Within the potential madhouse of contemporary society, he implores us to be reasoned and sane.

One may ask whether the frustration of not being listened to could result in an act of suicide, but such a question is for the psychiatrist, not the literary investigator. What we do know is that the injunction to communicate was stronger in Levi than in most writers. Acting as a conscientious witness gave supreme purpose to his life and more significantly, helped assuage his survivor's guilt. It is probably no coincidence that in his last book, the chapter entitled "Shame," is followed by the one entitled "Communicating."

Those writers who witnessed Europe's darkness and who speak of the failure of modern art to anticipate, understand or warn against the catastrophe,(one thinks here of Czselaw Milosz and Elias Canetti), they are the ones most laden with shame, most burdened with the responsibility to answer for what they write — as the Bible says — "Word by word, line by line, precept by precept." Their lucidity is the result of a style burnished by dire historical forces. What they have witnessed has given them little use for writing that is unclear or pretentious. In an essay entitled "On Obscure Writing," Levi lashes out against the contemporary writer who in his self-indulgence "cries in the desert, moans, laughs, sings and howls." But "noise is not sound," he tells us. "I'm tired of 'semantic refusals' and stale innovations. Blank pages are blank, and it is best to call them blank." He connects Ezra Pound's obscure poetry to his inability to think clearly and to his fascist politics. Most perplexing for us, he also links obscure writing to suicide: "It is not by chance that the two least decipherable poets writing in German, Trakl and Celan, both died as suicides... the obscurity of their poetry (is) a pre-suicide, a not-wanting-to-be, a flight from the world." He reserves, however, special sensitivity for Celan, a fellow survivor:

> Celan's obscurity is neither contempt for the reader, nor expressive inadequacy, nor lazy abandonment to the flow of the unconscious: it truly is a reflection of the obscurity of his fate and his generation... the darkness grows from page to page...it attracts us as chasms attract us.

One wonders if Levi is speaking here of the future chasm — the stairwell in his apartment building through which he plummeted to his death; one wonders if the injunction to write clearly was not only for his readers but to ward off those Furies which he confessed had pursued him through time. Yet we are left with a puzzle, for if Levi is correct in believing that Celan's dark and obscure poetry was his suicide note, then what do we make of Levi's own note, so reasoned, clear, and precise?

The unlistened-to story may have been Levi's nightmare, but it is apparent that in the camp and in the years following, he worked to make certain he did not live it. His literary output, considering he held a full-time job in industry, is notable as is the fact that he began writing his first book in the year after his liberation. The same confidence in a potential listener cannot be attributed to Levi's interlocutor, the shadow figure behind *The Drowned And The Saved*, the Austrian-born philosopher, Jean Améry. Améry, the author of a searing collection of essays entitled, *At The Mind's Limits*, avoided the subject of Auschwitz until 1964, when he was asked to give a lecture on a German radio programme. From the beginning, he is doubtful of the possibilities of changing those who need changing, of awakening those less conscious, those morally inferior. He is like a speaker who at any moment, in disgust and exasperation, might leave the podium. He feels, at times, absurd talking about his experiences and ashamed for being paid to do so. As he puts it: "What dehumanized me has become a commodity, which I offer for sale."

One should think of Améry as the post-Holocaust master of alienation. His subjects are homelessness, the loss of selfhood, the intellectual in an unresponsive world. His Jewish father died when he was young leaving him only a photograph of a man in a military uniform. His mother was Roman Catholic. He grew up completely devoid of Jewish tradition, thus he was unable in later years to connect with that tradition since in his mind "no one can become what he cannot find in his memories." For Améry, authenticity is all. And dignity. He relates his Jewishness to his victimization (he was tortured by the Gestapo and survived a succession of camps). He comes to the realization that dignity is understanding one's fate and revolting against it. In 1935, as he is sitting in a Vienna coffeehouse studying the Nuremberg Laws, Améry hears his "death sentence." He knows then that every Jew is "a dead man on vacation." In 1938 he emigrates to Belgium and from his original name (Hans Maier) he constructs a French anagram — Jean Améry. He joins the Resistance and adopts the philosophical position of "trading blows with the enemy." Even before the camps, he realizes that he has been deprived of home — not just his physical home (Vienna) but his deeper home: German language and culture. Speaking of the special difficulties of the Jewish intellectual of German educational and cultural background, he states: "No matter to what he turned, it did not belong to him, but to the enemy. Beethoven. But he was being conducted in Berlin by Furtwangler, a respected official of the Third Reich."

Although many differences exist between Améry and Levi, it is both striking and discomfiting to appreciate that in his last book, Primo Levi appears to have arrived, after forty-two years of enquiry, at a position not unlike Améry's. Their similarity is not a shared rage as Ozick has suggested and as perhaps Levi led her, unwittingly, to believe. For Levi tells us that he believes Améry's desire to "trade blows," his "severity and intransigence" made him "incapable of finding joy in life" and may offer one interpretation for his suicide. Yet most of Levi's chapter on Améry deals not with rage but with the questions of self in relation to language, culture, beliefs.

In any event a careful reading reveals that rage and revenge are not at the heart of Améry's despair, though he freely admits that they are passions he holds. According to him, any camp survivor who does not hold them is either insane or a masochist. However, the moral dimension of *At The Mind's Limits* comes in the form of the question: How is this rage and revenge to be undone? As it turns out, the S.S. man who beat Améry at Auschwitz is later executed. Yet this does not appease Améry, for rather than simple revenge, he wishes that the SS man, as he stood before the firing squad, "experienced the moral truth of his crimes ... I would like to believe that at the instant of his execution he wanted exactly as much as I to turn back time, to undo what had been done." This moral turning-back of the clock would turn the "antiman" into his "fellow man." To have the perpetrators of the crime against him and others realize and acknowledge their immorality — only that would undo the deed, redeem both victim and victimizer, "eradicate the ignominy." Améry expects no less from the entire German nation, and he believes his resentments serve the historical function of reminding Germans of the need to acknowledge their crimes. At the same time he knows this is

Primo Levi and The Unlistened-to-Story

impossible. That is what makes, *At The Mind's Limits*, such a disturbing book. Améry is one of those thinkers who spares himself and his reader nothing. "Whoever was tortured stays tortured," he tells us, and that which would undo the pain — admission and moral regeneration on the part of the perpetrators and their heirs — is an impossibility. Hence, the futility of speaking:

> But such a murder of millions as this... will be lumped with the bloody expulsion of Armenians or with the shameful acts of violence by the colonial French: as regrettable, but in no way unique. Everything will be submerged in a general "Century of Barbarism." We, the victims, will appear as the truly incorrigible, irreconcilable ones, as the antihistorical reactionaries...

Levi's designation of Améry as "a skeptic and pessimist by nature" is probably accurate. However, he respects Améry's lucidity, his unflinching inquisitiveness before the darkest questions, his desire to know. As Améry says of Auschwitz: "...nowhere else in the world did reality have as much effective power as in the camp, nowhere else was reality so real." At the same time he states — and this is the key to the essential difference between the two men — "In no other place did the attempt to transcend it (reality) prove so hopeless and so shoddy."

Both Améry and Levi agree that Auschwitz was a place where the intellectual was at a disadvantage. Attempting to make sense out of a senseless world, to understand a place that is not understandable, proved to be a waste of energy and a detriment to survival. But if the intellectual in Levi was at a disadvantage in Auschwitz, the artist and scientist were not. These facets helped both to connect and to distance him from life there in a way that was denied Améry, who seems to subscribe to Adorno's famous dictum: "No poetry after Auschwitz." In "The Canto of Ulysses" chapter from *Survival In Auschwitz*, Levi attempts to share the profundity and beauty of Dante's *Inferno* with a young French inmate. Communication is difficult because he must speak in broken French, but the little that does occur fills him with pleasure and meaning and more importantly, a sense of self. He views the event as a victory over the Nazi dehumanization, as a link to the world of culture and to his own past. In a similar situation, Améry has almost the opposite reaction. Noticing a flag waving atop a building in the camp, he recalls a favourite poem by Holderlin:

> I repeated the stanza somewhat louder, listened to the words sound, tried to track the rhythm, and expected that the emotional and mental response that for years this Holderlin poem had awakened in me would emerge. But nothing happened. The poem no longer transcended reality.

It is noteworthy that Levi's event involves another, that his joy is, in large part, tied to his ability to share what he feels and thinks. Améry, on the other hand, is alone with his thoughts. "The intellectual was alone with his intellect ... The experience of persecution was, at the very bottom, that of extreme loneliness."

Levi never expresses such hopelessness. This is partly due to his connection to language. In the Lager, Italian, unlike German, was not debased, thus Levi was able to preserve his cultural home. It is also apparent that in Auschwitz, Levi's physical suffering was less than Améry's. Moreover, the scientist in Levi encouraged dispassion while the artist in him could not subscribe to the absolute uselessness of art in the Lager, expressed so succinctly in Améry's caustic aphorism: "No bridge led from death in Auschwitz to *Death In Venice*." To a certain degree Levi concurs with Améry. He states: "Reason, art, and poetry are no help in deciphering a place from which they are banned." They may not help to decipher, but as the Dante episode indicates, they help to counteract. Levi was too much the poet to be overtaken by the negating stance. Believing in the redemptive power of art, he affirms Nietzsche's paradoxical epigram: "We have Art in order that we may not perish from Truth." And not just any art, for Levi's does seek epiphany, illumination. As he writes in his essay on Kafka: "In my writing ... I've always strived to pass from the darkness into the light, as a filtering pump might do, which sucks up turbid water and expels it decanted."

This explains why Levi, as Ozick states, "appears to be the one (Holocaust writer) who least troubles, least wounds, least implicates, the reader." Appears is the key word here, for Levi does not grab the reader by the lapels; he discomforts those who choose

Primo Levi and The Unlistened-to-Story

to be discomforted. Coventry Patmore said, "The end of art is peace," and I take his statement to be a comment on the artistic process. For no matter how disturbing, art is a transcending event, akin in nature to the religious. It is a healing occurrence. This may explain why Levi became a favourite with intellectuals: whatever unresolved feelings they may have about the Holocaust or anti-Semitism, in reading Levi, they are permitted to forgive themselves through his art. Améry's work permits no such loophole. It is too stark and unremitting to allow such a release.

This discussion raises the old, persistent question: Is art, like religion, an illusion, a romanticization, an avoidance of reality? Levi's art seems to me anything but. It believes in transcendence, yet knows that much of the surrounding world is set against it. It often assumes an ironic stance, or understated condemnation. And yet, because it is art, it is congenial. We can assimilate it. And perhaps disregard it.

Victor Frankl, in *Man's Search For Meaning*, tells us that in the camps the best all died while the worst survived. Such a self-condemnation is probably extreme but is repeated by both Levi and Améry. It pertains to the reality of quotas in the camps: if your number was on the list of the doomed it could be removed through bribery, favours, and other forms of manipulation, but some other number would have to replace it.

In reading through the work of Levi, one is aware that his guilt and shame increased with time. In his earlier books there is a muted sense of pride in his survival; he feels that the camp experience made him a writer and gave him a deeper understanding of human nature. However, it also gave him a responsibility to those who did not survive.

And what if the witness/writer is not listened to, or more in keeping with Améry's equation, what if he is made to feel doubly guilty by his persistence in speaking long after the rest of the world has forgotten? What if he is told, as Améry was by one German letter-writer: "...We are finally sick and tired of hearing again and again that our fathers killed six million Jews."

Levi checks his memory and finds no "obvious transgressions." Yet there is the shadow of suspicion "that each man is his brother's Cain, that each one of us has usurped his neighbour's place... It is a supposition that gnaws at us..."

It is with the book, *Moments of Reprieve* (1981), that Levi first uses these lines from Coleridge's, "The Rime of the Ancient Mariner," as an epigraph — lines that will surface again, as the epigraph to his last book, *The Drowned And The Saved*:

> *Since then, at an uncertain hour,*
> *That agony returns,*
> *And till my ghastly tale is told*
> *This heart within me burns.*

As if to stress their significance, Levi also used these lines to head "The Survivor," a poem which leads the reader back to the Lager-inferno and ends with Levi telling his death-in-life companions, "It's not my fault if I live and breathe, /Eat, drink, sleep and put on clothes."

Here is Coleridge's Mariner:

> *All stood together on the deck*
> *For a charnel-dungeon fitter:*
> *All fixed on me their stony eyes*
> *That in the Moon did glitter.*
>
> *The pang, the curse, with which they died*
> *Had never passed away:*
> *I could not draw my eyes from theirs,*
> *Nor turn them up to pray.*

It is fitting that in the end, a literary sensibility as refined and unique as Levi's would attach itself to myth: the archetype of the Ancient Mariner. Like the Mariner, Levi has been given the task to arrest, disturb and teach, and like the Mariner, his respite from suffering is only temporary. For unlike other poems that deal with the theme of re-creation through destruction, in Coleridge's the rebirth brought about is less powerful than the horror from which it has sprung. It is the haunting terror of the destructive experience that remains the dominant theme in the reader's mind.

Coleridge's poem is not only powerful but also puzzling; critics have long debated the meaning of the albatross. By murdering it, the Mariner sets in motion the nightmare he is to live out. At the same time his killing the bird seems gratuitous, unprovoked. And what does the bird symbolize? Interpretations are many, but I have found George Whalley's particularly convincing; he asserts that the albatross is Poetic Imagination, and in particular, Coleridge's. If what the Mariner has killed is his own poetic impetus, and if that is what sets off the hell he is consigned to live, then this may explain, at a symbolic level, the unfortunate turn which Levi's journey took. He, who had discovered a convincing style to relate his Holocaust experience, felt in the end that he had had no effect on the conscience of the perpetrators. This is emphasized in his final chapter: "Letters From Germans," and in the book's "Conclusion," where Levi tells us that his story has "become ever more extraneous as the years pass."

After forty-two years of telling his ghastly tale, Levi, like the Mariner, though saved and not drowned, found himself increasingly "alone on a wide wide sea." He who had suffered at the hands of others continued to suffer, and the telling of his tale to the World which, like Coleridge's Wedding-Guest, was at best a reluctant listener, brought only temporary, personal relief. Given the weight of responsibility that Levi had accepted as a writer, such a personal motive was, in any event, unacceptable. Eventually, he joined that phantom crew whose eyes continue to ask us the impossible questions.

CZESLAW MILOSZ:
THE WITNESS OF POETRY

For in reality, no man today can be a writer, a Dichter, *if he does not seriously doubt his right to be one.*

— Elias Canetti

Czeslaw Milosz was born in Lithuania, at Vilnius, in 1911. He is both unfortunate and fortunate to have lived through the two most significant historical events of our century: German and Soviet totalitarianism. Unfortunate for obvious reasons; fortunate because these experiences have given his work an authority and weight missing in that of most West European and North American authors.

He was educated in Lithuania and Paris, and studied law. During the war he was a writer and editor for underground resistance publications in Warsaw. What he witnessed in that shattered city confirmed the apocalyptic tone and imagery of the poems he had written before the war, when he had been part of the Catastrophe movement; it strengthened his belief that poetry is about "last things," connecting "one human life with the time of all humanity." Starting in 1946 he was a Polish diplomat, first in Washington, then in Paris, where in 1951 he broke with his government. Since 1960 he has been a professor of Slavic studies at the University of California.

Milosz has gone past the borders of poetry: he has written novels and essays whose subjects include politics, religion, mysticism, history, and poetics. He helps his reader along, trying to explain the state of his soul in relation to the various social and political climates he has encountered. As he says in *The Land of the Ulro*:

"Life is short, and I am attracted less and less to a literature which is self-consciously literary. The degree to which a work is of extra-literary importance is determined by the power of a given author's philosophy, that is, by the passion with which it is engaged with ultimate things, resulting in an extreme tension between the art and the thought."

Art and thought, the poet and the philosophizing essayist, imagination and reason, prophecy and understanding, Jerusalem and Athens: these are the poles of his world.

In a poem he tells us that the knows he will be remembered as "An item in the fourteenth volume of an encyclopaedia/ Next to a hundred Millers and Mickey Mouse." Though he would deny any claim to greatness, making disclaimers is essential to his paradoxical nature. He has achieved his largeness by proclaiming smallness; he has produced a formidable body of poetry under the guise of "anti-poetry." Both ascetic and sensual, faithless and believing — in his own words, "an ecstatic pessimist" — his sensibility is like a pendulum, driven by that consuming modern characteristic, contradiction.

Because his work is far-reaching in its desire to get at the large questions, he is not an easy author to discuss in total. There is, for instance, his political thought conveyed through the portraits and narratives that comprise *The Captive Mind*(1955); there are his views on the relationship between poetry and millennialism, in his Harvard lectures, *The Witness of Poetry*(1983); and then there is the evolution of the poetry itself, from the dark intense lyricism of his Catastrophe and World War II stage, to the more spacious, ruminative poems of recent years (see his *Collected Poems,* 1988).

In *The Land of Ulro,* his most recent and most philosophical prose work, Milosz gives us the names that have been most important to his spiritual development:

"Only now do I discern the thread joining the various phases of and influences on my mind's progress: Catholicism, Stanislaw Brzozowski, Oscar Milosz, Hegelianism, Swedenborg, Simone Weil, Shestov, Blake. The thread is my anthropocentrism and my bias against Nature."

This began with his interest in Manichaeism, a religion that combines the Christian theory of salvation and the Zoroastrian concept of dualism: the enmity, and equality, between light and darkness, good and evil. What is so heretical about this system is the idea that God, in some part, is imperfect or malevolent — or both. How, asked Mani and his followers, could such a miserable world have emanated from a creator who is good? Manichaean thought has constantly challenged the accepted Christian justifications of God, which posit a harmony and deny Mani's doctrine that there is a severe contradiction between hostile Matter and spiritual redemption. Manichaeism has a role in Christianity somewhat like the one that Kabbalah plays in Judaism, where it challenges the rationalism of Talmudic teaching.

Milosz calls modern man "neo-Manichaean": neo, because science has made it all but impossible to believe in grace and redemption, the traditional exits from the pain of confronting Nature. He uses the term "to describe our characteristic resentment of evil Matter to which we desperately oppose value, but value no longer flowing from a divine source and now exclusively human." Values — or so Nietzsche taught us — are merely extensions of man's will and as such are relative. Against Nature we have posed Reason, that is Science, but this has done little to alleviate our anxieties or fulfil our deep longings. Reality is hard to bear. And the question left to Man is how to transcend that reality, or transmute it.

Of the names on Milosz's "thread," the two most crucial to his dilemma and its attempted resolution are Simone Weil and William Blake. His intellectual development is like a movement from her to him.

Milosz has translated Weil into Polish, and wrote an essay called "The Importance of Simone Weil" in 1960. References to her work appear often in his prose and poetry. He has been drawn to it by the honesty and simplicity of her style, which he describes as "classical, dry, concise," and her power through that honesty to provoke "a salutary shame." Shame is an important element for Milosz, and is in fact the cause of the sparse, unadorned style he employs. Here for example is the opening stanza of "Dedication," one of his strongest poems, written in Warsaw in 1945:

> *You whom I could not save*
> *Listen to me.*
> *Try to understand this simple speech*
>   *as I would be ashamed of another.*
> *I swear, there is in me no wizardry of words.*
> *I speak to you with silence like a cloud or a tree.*

The poem is addressed to the dead; the tension in the poem comes from the poet's self-imposed responsibility. It is his task to speak clearly, unromantically, not to delude through language; for language itself is suspect, thanks to the linguistic extravagancies of pre-war writers, or to the deliberate perversion of language used in propaganda.

Milosz respects the moral courage of Simone Weil. He says she was "tactless in her writings and completely indifferent to fashions, able to go straight to the heart of the matter." The most significant offshoot of such courage is the ability to bear the tensions of our contradictory existence. For Milosz, Weil is the person most representative of Manichaen thought in our time, exemplifying "the contradiction between our longing for the good and the cold universe." Human beings find it hard, or impossible, to sustain contradictory thought. Most will not acknowledge it; others try to resolve it through systems: religious, political, scientific. Milosz commends Weil's efforts in this direction, which were "dictated toward making the contradiction as acute as possible." Through Weil, he chastises people who "practise the dialectical art by changing it into an art of compromises and who buy the unity of the opposites too cheaply."

If Milosz has an aesthetic and moral imperative it is this: not to buy the unity of the opposites too cheaply — if at all. In all of his writing he is a man who carries inside himself a chaos of contradictory things, yet at the same time the reader is aware that he does not approve of this chaos, that he does not feel at ease about it, that he is constantly trying to overcome it. He relentlessly goads poetry, questions it, as if to exact from it the moral significance he wishes it to have. In "Dedication" he asks "What is poetry which does not save/ Nations or people?" He would find it repulsive to passively accept Auden's notion that "poetry makes nothing happen," but he would not flinch from considering such a judgement. At the same time he refuses to concede to art a full-blown romantic role or to allow it to preen its feathers behind a closed door marked "art for art's sake." Poetry must not rest; it is, for him, a dialectical questioning that questions its own right to exist. Besides, there are other forces — historical, spiritual, and ethical — that can supersede art. In a recent poem called "1945," Milosz is reunited with a Polish poet "from the Avant-Garde," who had survived the war and who now "understood":

He could not have learned those things from Apollinaire,
Or Cubist manifestos, or the festivals of Paris streets.
The best cure for illusions is hunger, patience, and obedience.

Before 1939, artists for the most part used the daemonism, the irrationality of art to attack a civilization they judged to be hypocritical and vapid. Did that make them into accomplices of the irrational forces that overtook nations and led to cataclysm? So Simone Weil believed, and Milosz goes further, adding another overwhelming contradiction to his work: the primitive and irrational source of poetry may be one and the same as the source of more destructive historical elements. In the ironically named "Ars Poetica?" we come upon lines like these: "In the very essence of poetry there is something indecent" and "What reasonable man would like to be a city of demons?" The poem ends,

What I'm saying here is not, I agree, poetry,
as poems should be written rarely and reluctantly,
under unbearable duress and only with the hope
that good spirits, not evil ones, choose us for their instrument.

What can he mean by saying this is not poetry? Is he being perversely ironic? Does he mean it is not what we are used to as poetry, in that it reads, like much of his work, like an argument, an elegant essay? He disobeys Yeats's rule that the poet should not explain himself, just as he ignores Pound's imagist dictates. "Ars Poetica?" links poetry with "good spirits, not evil ones." This is such a distant notion that here it seems refreshingly new. We have lived for so long with the notion that the poet is a renegade, an iconoclast, and a parasite, that the idea that he may be aligned with the protection and preservation of civilization is a welcome change. But it is more than that. Behind the poem are the rubble of Warsaw and the ashes of Humanism, and his tone is an attempt to rebuild and resuscitate.

The tension between the irrational and the civilized, between the pagan and the Judaeo-Christian, is not the only one that Milosz bears. Although he is fond of quoting Simone Weil's epigram, "Contradiction is a lever of transcendence," it is not clear how that transcendence is to come about in her world except by a passive awaiting of grace. Her approach relies heavily on the speculative, Greek component in Christianity, at the expense of the Jewish, prophetic element. She was, after all, a philosopher, not a poet, and Milosz expresses his discomfort in her realm at the end of his essay "The Importance of Simone Weil," calling her an "Ariel," himself a "Caliban," "too fleshy, too heavy, to take on the feathers of an Ariel." But he does not rejoice in his creatureliness. There is a sense that he disapproves of it (twenty years later he says in a poem: "I was afraid of what was wild and indecent in me"), since it prevents him from taking flight from this world.

Milosz wrote "Shestov or the Purity of Despair" thirteen years after his essay on Weil (both are in *The Emperor of Earth,* 1977). It is an important essay in understanding the development of Milosz's thought. Like Weil, Lev Shestov was a great paradoxalist; his despair is pure because it cannot be reconciled. But the essential difference between Weil and Shestov is far more important than the similarities. Shestov, who is unwilling to retreat from this world, who refuses to abandon his dialogue with a God who has withdrawn, is far more of a humanist and a Jewish thinker than Weil. Above all, he does not wish to annihilate the "I"; his world is more personal, subjective; less Greek.

Milosz intuits that this is the central problem with Weil's approach. He asks, "Why should we hate 'I'? Was it not the 'I' of Job that complained and wailed? Was not the God who would demand such an impossible detachment from us a God of philosophers rather than a God of prophets?" Milosz makes a distinction here between the philosophic and prophetic traditions that has tremendous consequences for our age. In *The Republic*, Socrates talks of a philosophic man confronting a furious mob. The man is without confederates who could help maintain justice and therefore he feels as if he were surrounded by beasts. Socrates tells us that henceforth this man will keep silent, attend to his own work, become a spectator of society. To appreciate a central difference between the Greek and Hebraic traditions, we can compare this detached observer with the enraged and relentless Isaiah, compelled to speak his message, who in Blake's words "cares not for consequences."

I think this particular tension is predominantly a Christian one. Our age may be Manichaean, Gnostic, Kabbalistic in its approach to experience, but the despair resulting from Man's distrust of Nature never reaches the intensity in Judaism that it does in Christianity. Moreover, the desire to retreat radically from this world is antithetical to Judaism. Here is Martin Buber on Simone Weil:

"When she referred to the God of Israel as a 'natural' God and to that of Christianity as a 'supernatural' God, she failed entirely to understand the character of the former inasmuch as he is not 'natural' but is the God of nature as well as the God of spirit — and is superior to both nature and spirit alike. But even if Simone Weil had known the true God of Israel, she would not have been satisfied, for he turns toward nature, which he dominates, whereas Simone Weil sought flight from nature. Reality had become intolerable to her, and for her, God was the power that led her away from it. But that is definitely not the way of the God of Israel; such a way would be the very opposite of his relation toward his creation and his creatures. He has placed man in the centre of reality in order that he should face up to it."

Buber also dissents from Weil's wish to annihilate the "I" since, as he states, "the real relationship taught by Judaism is a bridge which spans across two firm pillars, man's 'I' and the 'I' of his eternal partner."

Even in Kabbalah, the most Manichaen-like of Jewish writings, the evil of matter is not to be turned away from. For in the final stage of the Kabbalist myth there is *Tikkun*: a restoration of the world, which must be carried out in *this* world as well as in Man's inner world. Hasidism, a later phase of Jewish mystical teaching goes further: Personal redemption comes through the very process of restoration in this world; one loves one's neighbour not solely to be a good person, but because it is only through such an act that we come to know God.

Does this retreat-from-the-world notion, embedded in the Platonic spectator story, account in part for the silence of many Christian intellectuals and church officials during the Holocaust? In one of Milosz's most powerful wartime poems, "A Poor Christian Looks At The Ghetto," the poet sees himself as the failed Christian ("poor" in spirit), burrowing through the debris of the Jewish ghetto, watched by a mole whom he imagines to be a Jewish patriarch. "What will I tell him," Milosz asks, "I, a Jew of the New Testament?" fearful that, "he will count me among the helpers of death:/The uncircumcised." The title emphasizes "Looks," and we are left feeling that the poet condemns Christians for refusing to be Isaiahs, for choosing to be spectators — either out of cowardice or due to a mode of thinking. In these wartime poems Milosz's repeated judgement is that he and his generation were decadent, apathetic, and opportunistic. From this, perhaps, the "salutary shame" he suggests in his essay on Weil.

But because he is a powerful poet, Milosz, in the final analysis, stands not as a spectator, but as a witness. The difference is one of responsibility. The witness stands, after the crime, in some court (in the case of a writer, probably his own) and testifies to the historical truth, which very often turns out to be the truth about himself.

All of the tensions I have discussed so far lead Milosz to the last name on the "thread": Blake. William Blake shares honesty and courage with Simone Weil. She was "completely indifferent to fashion, violent in her judgements, and uncompromising," and Blake, according to T. S. Eliot, "approached everything with a mind unclouded by current opinions. Eliot adds, "This makes him terrifying." Like Weil, Blake is committed to the law of contradiction. In "The Marriage of Heaven and Hell" he writes, "Without Contraries is no progression" and by progression we understand not just spiritual progress but poetic movement too. Yet the essential difference for Milosz is that while Weil's supplicant has turned from the world to await grace, Blake's bard actively redeems himself through imaginative pursuits that fuse Reason and Desire. Milosz says:

"A revolt against Nature does not, in Blake, imply a yearning for an ideal realm. On the contrary, his Garden of Eden is earth; his source of heavenly pleasure, the five senses; his salvation, the eternal *now*, and not some tomorrow beyond the sunset of life."

In Blake's cosmology, Milosz has found a way to preserve Weil's dictum — to bear the contradictions — and at the same time embrace, not renounce, the present. And though he cannot resolve the tensions, he can, through Blake's notion of Imagination, transmute them by a process that embodies intelligence and love. Through artistic creativity he can for a moment transcend the chaos inflicted by the contradictions — an idea not peculiar to Blake. Frost, for instance, thought of the poem as "a momentary stay against confusion." Yeats believed that when he created a poem he was creating his self out of the daily "bundle of accident and incoherence."

In *The Land of Ulro* (Ulro is Blake's term for the spiritual wasteland), this awareness does not move Milosz to joyous proclamation or scathing denouncement. The tone of the book is dispassionate, ironic, and self-analytic; its author is an inhabitant of the spectral purgatory he wishes to transcend. He tells us that he has "surrendered to the law of Imagination" — but that implies resignation, not an exuberant taking-hold. For it to be otherwise, would Milosz have to belong to another century? Or to put it another way: What poet today, taking the high tones of a prophet, would be listened to? Milosz is admirable for his tenacious tentativeness, his honesty in not jumping at the easy resolution to his dilemma. And for his unceasing scepticism.

We come long after Blake. What he intuited — the problem that Science and disembodied Reason would present for the human Imagination — was reassessed at the end of the last century by Nietzsche. We still live in the shadow of that philosopher's world: the death of God, the vanishing of horizons, the relativity of values. In such a world the permanence of poetry disappears as well. When man decided his soul was not immortal, he began to believe his work — culture— *was*. That belief too has gone by the wayside. Language is one of the earliest and deepest horizons, the one out of which God springs ("In the Beginning was the Word"); and so it is the last to go. The despair that results is, quite literally, almost unspeakable. I know of no poem that presents this so incisively as this one by Paul Celan (translated by Michael Hamburger):

> *To stand in the shadow*
> *of the scar up in the air.*
> *To stand-for-no-one-and-nothing.*
> *Unrecognized,*
> *for you*
> *alone.*
> *With all there is room for in that,*
> *even without*
> *language.*

How shall we respond to this awareness? What tone shall we take? Artists after the First World War intensified their attacks on a civilization they called corrupt, making use of extreme irrationality in movements like Dadaism and Surrealism. After the cataclysm of the Second World War, Samuel Beckett projected a cosmic sneer over the spiritual impotence of two paralysed vaudevillians. Painters offered black canvases, and philosophers questioned the right of poets to sing in the wake of annihilation. In the continued anti-rationalism and nearly complete pessimism of many post-war artists one heard an "I-told-you-so" tone.

With Milosz we hear a new voice. I believe he is a man who would like to have praised, and occasionally he has; but mostly he is a poet who prays. He is Man expectant, standing in the present tense, willing to bear the pain of reality, yet beseeching. In his beautiful poem, "On Angels," he tenderly invokes these winged messengers and, in the dark of our century's horrors, asks them to "do what you can." In this, one sees a step away from Beckett's absurdist laughter. And who can tell if the day will not come when a poet again may praise radiant creatures. Or wrest from them a name.

SCHINDLER'S LIST : REEL HISTORY

And if thou bring forth the precious out of the vile, thou shalt be as my mouth.

— Jer. 15:19

He who tells the story of a righteous one draws the light of the Messiah into the world and expels much of the darkness.

— Rabbi Nachman of Brazlav.

As a subject for filmmakers, the Holocaust has proven to be a gorgon. Those who deal with it too directly, lacking the shield of guile and craft, are destined to see their work plummet onto the stone-heap of failed productions. One has only to think of the embarrassingly poor television film *Holocaust,* or some of the less convincing camp scenes from *Sophie's Choice* to understand that this is largely a problem of depiction. By stating this I am admitting my belief that the Holocaust is a permissible subject for art, even the art of film. This is a view not shared by everyone, for movies have a marked tendency to trivialize events, not even sparing those that demand the utmost seriousness.

This explains why many of the better filmmakers decide not to *show* the Holocaust at all. In *The Garden Of the Finzi-Continis*, the Holocaust becomes a background to all that is happening, a presence between the lines of dialogue, informing the actors' gestures and glances. In Lanzmann's brilliant documentary, *Shoah*, depiction is rigorously avoided. As in a Greek tragedy, the violence has been committed off-stage. The testimony of the witnesses, both survivors and perpetrators, stands naked as the silence of the camera draws us into the enormity of the horror.

Those filmmakers who have succeeded with depiction have done so because their work is highly stylized. In Lina Wertmuller's *Seven Beauties,* the scenes of Auschwitz are purposely unrealistic; they resemble paintings — her corpses reminiscent of Michelangelo's nude studies, her muted umbers and blues taken from Renaissance canvasses. Some find such an approach irreverent, but this type of stylization has the effect of drawing one away from the direct glare of the awesome subject. In the case of *Seven Beauties*, this deflection actually enhances Wertmuller's motif. Her intent is to remind us of the Renaissance (the birth of European humanism) in the midst of Auschwitz (the death of that humanism).

It is my belief that Steven Spielberg has also chosen stylization as the means of treating this subject, and that he has chosen a stylization so ingenious that a number of film critics have praised the realism of *Schindler's List*. The film, however, is anything but realistic. It is, to a large degree, accurate. (We know, for instance, that Spielberg had S.S. uniforms made for the film and then declined to use them, searching instead throughout Germany until he was able to find the actual thing.) This accuracy was needed to create the sense of documentary. There are certain periods in history that we are familiar with through photographs or film. For instance, we *know* Victorian England through a certain style of photography and David Lynch made use of that to create authenticity in his *Elephant Man*. Likewise, most of us *know* the Holocaust through photographs and newsreel war footage. Despite the historical revisionists and Holocaust deniers, there is no doubt that these images have become a permanent part of our psychic landscape.

With *Schindler's List*, Spielberg has shown that a filmmaker can use these well-known images and simulate the sense of documentary to convince us that what we are watching is *real* history when in fact what we are responding to is *reel* history. The realism we speak of in reference to *Schindler's List* is our recognition of filmic material. Hence the artistic problem of depiction is solved for we are convinced that what we are viewing is truthful.

For a variety of reasons, *Schindler's List* is a landmark film, not the least of which is the fact that it undoes that profane, yet accomplished piece of cinematography, Leni Riefenstahl's *Triumph of The Will*. It is Spielberg's film that finally turns the tables on Riefenstahl's propaganda, a task which a number of critics previously suggested was accomplished by Hans-Jurgen Syberberg's *Our Hitler, a Film from Germany*. My opinion is that Syberberg's work is too verbose, pedantic and anti-cinematic to break the force and emotionalism of *Triumph of the Will*. In the end, Syberberg's hyper-intellectualization makes one wonder if the film isn't a device for avoiding, rather than confronting, his subject matter.

It is worth noting that both *Triumph of the Will* and *Schindler's List* mimic the documentary style: the former for the purpose of propaganda, the latter for artistic effect. There are still those who watch Riefenstahl's film of the Nuremberg Party Convention and believe they are viewing a documentary, rather than a carefully staged pseudo-documentary. One, after all, expects a documentary to be ingenuous and candid; *Triumph of the Will* is anything but. Riefenstahl herself has written: "The preparations for the Party Convention were made in concert with the preparations for the camera work." According to the film historian, Siegfried Kracauer, the Nazis saw the preparations for the convention in terms of a movie set production: "...grandiose architectural arrangements were made to encompass mass movements, and, under the personal supervision of Hitler, precise plans of the marches and parades had been drawn up long before the event... *Triumph of the Will* is undoubtedly the film of the Reich's Party Convention; however, the Convention itself had also been staged to produce *Triumph of the Will*..." It is altogether fitting, therefore, that Albert Speer who designed the buildings and site of the rally is listed in the film's credits as "architect." What we have here is an historical event planned and designed as the *mise en scene* for a film which is to be passed off as a documentary. Historical fig-

Schindler's List: Reel History

ures play at being actors. (It is documented that some of the Nazi heavyweights such as Rosenberg and Hess had their histrionic speech scenes re-shot weeks after the convention when it was discovered that some film footage had been ruined.) The intent of Riefenstahl's film is to confuse and deceive. In contrast, the last scene of *Schindler's List* in which each actor appears with the actual person he or she represented in the film, is intended to make us aware that what we have witnessed is a document, an homage, but not a documentary. Spielberg, as it were, discloses his cards and we slip from reel history to real history. (One might realize a final irony in this as the actor Neeson places a flower on Schindler's grave, considering that Oskar Schindler himself was one of life's most daring actors.) But aside from these considerations of authenticity, *Schindler's List* undoes *Triumph of the Will* because it is cinematically more powerful and because it, in effect, swallows the form of the former film. For despite Spielberg's use of documentary, it is not the film's overriding style.

There are a variety of styles at work in the film. Occasionally, as in the night club scene with Schindler and his wife, we seem to be in a grand Hollywood romance of the thirties. In the scene where Schindler is bartering for his female workers, the eyes of the Auschwitz administrator are covered in shadow, and we seem to be watching *film noir*. Spielberg is more of a synthesizer than an innovator, and *Schindler's List* is a film which makes use of other films without seeming derivative. The variety of styles and techniques makes the film essentially expressionistic. As Herbert Read points out in *The Meaning of Art*, "Expressionistic art is art that gives outward release to some inner pressure, some internal necessity." It seems that with *Schindler's List* Spielberg has found a subject of "some internal necessity." Hence his comment in *Time* magazine that in making the film he "felt liberated for the first time in my career."

In using the word "liberated" Spielberg connects with the great tradition of expressionistic film. Kracauer points out in his comprehensive study, *From Caligari To Hitler*, that Eisenstein's highly expressionistic cinema came about during that short period of true communism in Russia when a revolutionized people saw expressionism as a liberating force, combining "the denial of bourgeois traditions with faith in man's power freely to shape society and nature." Likewise, in the great period of German cinema that saw such classics as *The Cabinet of Dr. Caligari* and Fritz Lang's *Dr. Mabuse, the Gambler*, a similar attraction to expressionism was connected to the wish to be liberated from the physical and psychological devastation of W.W.I. With the possible exception of *Empire of the Sun,* Spielberg has spent his considerable talent producing fluff. With *Schindler's List* he has finally been liberated from the constraints of commercialism and juvenility. His career may tell us something about the role of the artist in America. It seems that in his late forties, Spielberg has grown up. One might say that by identifying with his Jewish tradition he has become 5,000 years old.

How does this act of liberation influence the artist's style? According to Read, the "inner pressure" he refers to "is generated by emotion, feeling, or sensation, and the work of art becomes a vent or safety-valve through which the intolerable psychic distress is restored to equilibrium. Such a release of psychic energy is apt to lead to exaggerated gestures..." Think of the opening night club scene, the way Schindler holds his cigarette, flashes money to the side of his head — a discreet waiter bends and accepts: whispers, sidelong glances, and Schindler's eyes, the eyes through which we will witness horror and compassion, sizing up his Nazi prey.

One might argue that the greatest films have been expressionistic. By that I mean films in which gesture is predominant, carrying meaning from the narrative over into the sublime, from language to the visually poetic. It is that which gives rise to what Roland Barthes, in his essay on Eisenstein, termed *the filmic* : "... that in the film which cannot be described, the representation which cannot be represented. The filmic begins only where language and metalanguage end."

This quality of *the filmic* would describe the greatest works in cinema: *The Cabinet of Dr. Caligari*, Eisenstein's *Ivan The Terrible* and *Potemkin*, Welles' *Citizen Kane* and *Touch of Evil*. I believe that a study of these films would indicate strong links to *Schindler's List*. For instance, it is fair to say that no one since Eisenstein in *Potemkin* has managed crowd scenes to such effect as Spielberg does here. (Think of the hand-held camera in the selection sequence, the parents running after the trucks which are carrying their children to certain death; or the faces between the slats of the cattle cars gasping for air; the storm-troopers, viewed from below, emptying the contents of suitcases over apartment balconies; the camera peering luridly through the bubble window of the gas-chamber door at the huddled naked women.)

Viewing the film as an expressionistic work allows us to give it the reading it deserves. Critics who viewed *Schindler's List* as a realistic *tour de force* objected to the last part of the film where Schindler, in their view, overreacts in a Dostoyevskian breakdown, lacerating himself for the fact that he did not save more Jews. But those who viewed the film in the light of expressionism completely understood those moving gestures of the large man doubled over with grief and the female prisoners huddling about him in a ring to give comfort.

Of course, as in all effective art, something more complex is at work. Throughout the film a creative tension exists between the expressionistic and documentary styles. The latter acts as the anchor for the film providing stability so that the expressionism can take flight. Generally speaking, there is something sober and understated about documentary. In *Schindler's List* it acts as a distancing device that puts a check on the artist's unquestionable passion and which controls the film's emotionalism. At times the expressive leaps out from the documentary; at other times, it is subdued. Usually they temper each other as in the scene in which the corpses from the ghetto massacre are being exhumed and incinerated. This is one of the scenes, directly imitative of documentary footage (the half-rotted corpses tossed onto smouldering pyres). In the midst of this destruction of evidence, an S.S. officer, in a fit of laughing madness, begins shooting into the burning pile of corpses. Had this scene not had the documentary set-up, his actions would surely have appeared to us as heavy-handed, overly dramatic.

Symbolism is not antithetical to expressionism and the film begins with a tableau that acts as a microcosm for the entire work. We have a humble family welcoming the Sabbath. Their humility is in contrast to the arrogance of the Nazis; their reverence for tradition, is in contrast to the Nazi scorn for the same. (Goeth will proudly tell his troops that they are about to wipe out centuries of history with their eradication of the Cracow ghetto.) The Sabbath blessing is for God's day of rest, yet the action of the film takes place in a work camp. As the flame of the last Sabbath candle is extinguished, smoke rises from the wick conjuring in the viewer's mind the smokestacks of the crematoria. Eisenstein, in his study *The Film Sense*, claims that the art of film-making deals not with *"representation"* but rather with that which "obliges spectators themselves to *create"* and thus "achieves that great power of inner creative excitement." As the camera lingers on the candle's smoke what is heard is a loud hiss. The viewer knows he is hearing a train's steam engine yet what he sees is the candle. "Art," according to Eisenstein, "begins the moment the creaking of a boot on the sound track occurs against a different visual shot and thus gives rise to corresponding associations." What is astonishing about watching *Schindler's List* is that it reminds us of the potential of film. At the same time it makes us aware of how impoverished most films are, how trivial in theme and unresourceful in technique.

Association can also be achieved through the process of repetition. In the opening scene we have two candles, and this sets the stage for the film's innumerable examples of doubling. The Sabbath scene itself will be repeated near the end of the film in Schindler's factory. When Schindler steps onto the streets of Cracow, something like snow is falling. He brushes it from his car hood and realizes it is ash from the corpse-burning taking place on the city's edge. Later, as the women arrive in Auschwitz, it again appears to be snowing but the viewer wonders whether it is ash from the crematorium smokestack. Goeth's botched execution of the hinge-maker is mirrored in his own nearly botched execution as the attendant kicks at the hangman's stool which will not topple over. The victims' gold teeth dropped callously before the prisoner-jeweler are counterpoised with the later gold tooth willingly donated to make the ring which will assist Schindler in his escape. The doubling here is unobtrusive and prompts not only creative but moral associations. For Goeth and Schindler are also doubles in the film. Their profiles and hairstyles bear an uncanny resemblance, and Spielberg is intent on drawing our attention to this in a scene that cuts back and forth between the two men shaving. As well, there are the later scenes

Schindler's List: Reel History

in which Goeth paws the body of Helen Hirsch, then beats her, inter-cut with scenes of a beautiful night club singer making overtures to Schindler. The confused, violent and aggressive man is counterpoised with the gentle man, deserving of woman's affection.

The danger of doubling is that it can lead to impressions of a simplistic moral world. *Schindler's List* manages to avoid this. The black and white style is not a metaphor for evil and good. After all, the predominant shade in a black and white film is grey — the predominant colour of any human being, and especially the shade of the German entrepreneur, Oskar Schindler. At the same time Spielberg's film has left no doubt as to its moral intent. This is what makes it such a refreshing work in an age when most films romanticize depravity, confuse obvious moral issues, or trivialize the human spirit. Part of the reason we weep at sections of *Schindler's List* is that it shows us that human beings can be good. It is as if we had forgotten that, as if in watching the film we were reclaiming that potential in ourselves. In the prologue to the novel, Keneally tells us "this is the story of the pragmatic triumph of good over evil, a triumph in eminently measurable, statistical, unsubtle terms." Yet when he goes on to state "... it is a risky enterprise to have to write of virtue," we should ask ourselves why? What is it in our culture that makes it so? When Stern holds up the list of names and says: "The list is absolute good — all around is the gulf," he is confronting much of contemporary culture that seems to dictate that ethics are strictly relative. To a large degree, Oskar Schindler's ethics *are relative*, yet he does know limits; after all, adultery is not rape, exploitation is not murder.

This leads us to another means of deflection: the story itself. Both the book and film are devoted to Oskar Schindler's story rather than that of the Holocaust. Story-telling has paramount significance in Judaism. Tales, parables, and anecdotes are not only intended to reveal wisdom but to keep tradition alive. Oskar Schindler's story was kept alive because a man he had saved, Leo Pfefferberg, told it one day to a customer in his luggage shop — the author, Thomas Keneally. Another thing about traditional narrative is that it implies rationality, order, cause and effect. It gleans this from the chaos of our lives. Schindler's story is a strong and gripping one and set against the irrationality of the Holocaust, conveys the moral intent of the artist. Within the story Schindler himself uses parable to reveal to Goeth what power is (not random terror, but the ability to be merciful) and the astonishing thing is that for a day or two the parable has its effect. Like a reborn emperor, Goeth walks around the camp, hand raised in a merciful Papal gesture, pardoning inmates. Then it is back to business as usual. Yet to have even a minimal effect on so deranged a character suggests the potential of story telling.

All the discussion that took place in the press after the film's debut about whether or not Oskar Schindler was a good or bad man, a true or mock hero, seems off the mark. To compare him, as some have done, to Janus Korczak, leads nowhere. The latter was a Jew, and as such, slated for death. His heroism was enacted within his very limited options. Schindler was a German who flirted with Nazism (not, it seems, for ideological reasons but for opportunistic ones). As a German entrepreneur his range of choices was far greater than Korczak's. This makes his decision to help the Jews mysterious and moving, for in this century we tend to think of evil as irrational. What this story seems to suggest is that it is goodness that may be inexplicable. Anyone who has read the detailed history of the Final Solution knows how the Germans turned death into a business: contracts to build the ovens, to supply the gas; women's hair woven into mattresses; ashes bagged as fertilizer. The film makes it abundantly clear how high-ranking Nazis profited from bribes, theft and larceny, how closely self-interest was tied to ideology.

What intensifies the mystery of Oskar Schindler is that he was a hedonist; in fact, it was his very hedonism that probably led to his moral decisions. This has perplexed some who have chastised Spielberg for presenting a tainted hero. Their saint is supposed to resemble Gandhi. Yet it is likely that the hedonistic personality may be as willing as the ideological or theological to defend goodness. Certainly in Schindler's case, because he was a man of action, he was in a better position to do so.

It is also possible that viewers are not aware of the historical facts. For instance, the film has Schindler arrested by the Gestapo once; in fact, he was arrested three times, and during the last he and those close to him fully expected he would be executed. Fur-

Schindler's List: Reel History

thermore, the film does not reveal an additional historical fact: namely, that Schindler was one of the first to provide objective (i.e. non-Jewish) testimony as to the destruction of European Jewry, testimony that reached the ears of high-ranking Allied politicians and administrators.

Though many viewers find the horror in the film difficult to take, the truth is that here, as with the documentary style and narrative, Spielberg has employed a shield to deflect the true horror of the event. In most instances the worst is not shown. In the Auschwitz shower scene gas does not come out of the faucet. After the women are rescued we see those who will not be saved descend into the chambers. Earlier in the film, when Stern is rescued from the cattle car, we witness the carloads of personal effects and the extracted teeth with gold fillings that remind us of those who were not saved. Steven Zaillian, the film's screenwriter, dedicated his Oscar to those who were *not* on Schindler's List, and it is obvious that throughout the film his intent was to point to these. As for the several characters who are shot in the head I will point to this. In his book on Auschwitz, *At the Mind's Limits*, the survivor Jean Améry tells us that the majority of inmates had accepted death as inevitable. What concerned people was not *if*, but rather, *how* they would die. One day, an S.S. officer, enraged by something Améry had done, dragged him out of the barracks and threatened to shoot him in the head. Améry says he had to conceal his relief, for according to him, this was the easiest death available in the camps. It is my belief that persons even mildly conversant with the literature of the Holocaust are aware as they watch the film that what they are witnessing is not the ultimate that took place there.

The film has certain specific Jewish references that a non-Jewish audience may not pick up, and I will conclude by remarking on two of them. Spielberg has made notable use of music in the film, most effectively in the two hand-held camera scenes: the liquidation of the Cracow ghetto and the selection sequence. In the former, as Schindler watches the massacre from a hilltop, the audience is listening to the strains of the Mark Warshavsky composition *By The Fireside* (*Oif'n Pritpetchik*), a classic Yiddish folksong. The lyrics (sung by a children's choir) tell us that a rebbe (teacher) sits by a fireside instructing his children in the learning of the *aleph-bet* (the alphabet). Much of diasporic life is packed into the song: the wish for a home, the importance of learning, the preciousness of children. The song tells us that the rebbe teaches by repetition and so the refrain is repeated, as are the killings on the cobblestone streets of Cracow. A little girl, tinted red, somehow manages to escape the slaughter and make her way to temporary safety. The scene is difficult to watch. Being familiar with the song's tradition and knowing its content makes it almost unbearable.

There is something else that has not been mentioned in any of the reviews that I have read, perhaps because it has a political overtone. Spielberg has included within his film an understanding of the link between the *Shoah* and the birth of Israel. All the actors playing Jews, with the exception of Ben Kingsley, are Israelis and the accents we hear are not Polish-Jewish but Israeli. This is as it should be since Israel is the phoenix that arose from the ashes of the Warsaw Ghetto fighters. Again, music has meaning. Near the end of the film, a sole Russian soldier approaches the factory to tell Schindler's Jews they have been liberated. They ask him where they should go. He advises them not to go to the East. "They hate you there," he says. (Many Jews who returned to their Polish towns were murdered in pogroms in the years *after* the war.) Likewise, he advises not to go West. "Isn't that a town over there?" he asks, pointing. The film cuts immediately to a wide-angle shot of Schindler's Jews coming over a hill singing *Jerusalem, City of Gold*.

The last scene, the homage at Schindler's grave, takes place in Jerusalem. That is where Oskar Schindler requested to be buried. From his venerated gravestone the camera's eye moves to the last doubling scene, the desecrated Jewish gravestones that the Nazis used to line the road to Goeth's camp. Over these, the list of credits rolls.

PERISHING THINGS AND STRANGE GHOSTS: RUPERT BROOKE'S LAST POEM

Rupert Brooke served as a naval officer in the First World War. Other than witnessing the evacuation of Antwerp, he saw no military action before he died of blood poisoning and dysentery two days before his ship was to arrive at Gallipoli. He was buried at night in an olive grove on the Greek island of Skyros. It was a poetic burial: his fellow officers have left accounts of rowing the dead poet to shore under the Aegean moon. To read their descriptions is heartbreaking, considering that most of them would be dead within two weeks.

After the war, the simple white cross that marked Brooke's grave was replaced with a hideous bronze statue, modeled after the Apollo Belvedere. The memorial was English society's way of securing Brooke within the myth it had created for him. As Philip Larkin rightly observed, "People had ideas about Brooke." But this was partly Brooke's own doing and the transformation of his grave to kitsch speaks not about Brooke's artistry, but about his aspirations and his relationship to the society he served.

What is apparent in the biographies and the letters is that Brooke was a young man working hard at promoting himself within the Edwardian literary establishment. He was charming and opportunistic. In the halcyon days before the First World War, he established a cozy life of comfort and connections. This comes across in the numerous photographs in Michael Hastings's biography, where the young poet and his circle are seen enjoying their hiking trips, horse rides, swim parties, and amateur theatrical ventures. It strikes us as a life of privilege and helps to convince us that Brooke, in contrast to some of his contemporaries, is historically irrelevant. The mannered literary world he inhabited was to be blown away by the haunting images we have been left of Owen, Rosenberg, post-war Graves and Sassoon, standing in grey and black contrast to the youth with blond waves and flashing blue eyes whom Yeats called "the handsomest man in England," and who would come to represent his countrymen's fallen Adonis.

Whether Brooke knew it or not, he played a dangerous game with his talent, one that would fossilize him for succeeding generations. In exchange for glamorization and applause, he was willing to serve English society. And be used by it. The Dean of St. Paul's was quoting Brooke's famous sonnet "The Soldier" as part of his Sunday sermon to drum up patriotic support and encourage enlistment at the same time that its author was sailing with the Hood Battalion toward his death in the Dardanelles. The exploitation would intensify in the weeks that followed. On April 23, 1915, only three days after Brooke's death, Winston Churchill, in a widely published, three page generic obituary, would use the dead poet as follows:

> ... he was willing to die for the dear England whose beauty and majesty he knew; and he advanced toward the brink in perfect serenity, with absolute conviction of the rightness of his country's cause, and a heart devoid of hate for fellow-men.

This myth of the good and wholesome man would persist long after the war. In 1955, Sir Geoffrey Keynes' attempt to bring out *The Letters of Rupert Brooke* was blocked by his fellow trustees of Brooke's estate (Walter de la Mare, Dudley Ward, John Sheppard); they claimed the collection "seriously misrepresented" Brooke. When the book finally appeared in 1968, the letters were censored and the collection was far from complete. One reviewer counted 300 excisions from 600 letters. Why the omissions? To deny Brooke's anti-Semitism or downplay the extent of his sexual

Perishing Things and Strange Ghosts

pursuits? To diminish his self-centredness and opportunism?

Christopher Hassall's detailed biography portrays a much more complex Brooke than the manufactured image suggests. He had a difficult relationship with his controlling mother (whom he referred to as "the Raj") and his tempestuous love affair with Ka Cox brought him to breakdown and near suicide. Those closest to him claim he often joked about his good looks and was skeptical about how people reacted to them. For instance, he reports after his meeting with Henry James: "I did the fresh boyish stunt, and it was a great success." Once, before a reading, he asks a friend: "Will you please disarrange my hair; I've got to read poetry to some old ladies." After a speech to The Arts and Letters Club in Toronto, he is approached by a young man who compliments him; his response: "Then I do my pet boyish-modesty-stunt and go pink all over, and everyone thinks it too delightful." If these comments reveal something distasteful and cynical about Brooke's personality, they also suggest he was aware of the image he was creating.

All of what I have written thus far is an attempt to disentangle the man from the myth because I want to comment on the poetry, which, by and large, is no longer regarded seriously. Since Brooke is perceived as a man who was on the "wrong side" in cultural and political matters, a retrospective irony haunts the reading of much of his work, especially his sonnet sequence "1914." None of his images has been picked upon more than the one in "Peace," in which he depicts new recruits as "swimmers into cleanness leaping," suggesting that enlistment is liberating these young men from "a world grown old and cold and weary." Paul Fussell, in his insightful study *The Great War And Modern Memory*, points out how Brooke's "swimmers" of 1914, "metamorphose into the mud-flounderers of the Somme and Passchendaele sinking beneath the surface." And it is highly probable that Wilfred Owen had Brooke's line in mind when he described soldiers who "Leapt to swift unseen bullets," or when he depicted death by mustard gas as death by drowning in his searing indictment "*Dulce et Decorum Est*."

I myself have used Brooke. Some years ago I taught a humanities course whose intent was to deal with major events of the twentieth century through literature. I employed Brooke's famous sonnet, "The Soldier" as a foil for Wilfred Owen's *"Dulce et Decorum Est."* Brooke's poem is a love sonnet, expressing love of nation, and for a liberal cosmopolitan, the values it espouses seem ludicrous, old-fashioned, class-conscious:

> *If I should die, think only this of me:*
> *That there's some corner of a foreign field*
> *That is forever England. There shall be*
> *In that rich earth a richer dust concealed;*
> *A dust whom England bore, shaped, made aware,*
> *Gave, once, her flowers to love, her ways to roam,*
> *A body of England's, breathing English air,*
> *Washed by the rivers, blest by suns of home.*

Against such lines, I set Owen's harrowing description:

> *Gas! Gas! Quick, boys! — An ecstasy of fumbling,*
> *Fitting the clumsy helmets just in time;*
> *But someone still was yelling out and stumbling*
> *And flound'ring like a man in fire or lime*

Juxtaposed to such eye-witnessed horrors, Brooke's unconditional willingness to die for his country, his sense of cultural superiority, his notion of antiseptic war-time killing, seem at least naïve, at worst, sacrilegious. I was using the image we have inherited of Brooke, the quaint, establishment poet, against the image we have of Owen, the truthful, rebel poet; or to reduce things even further, I was setting Brooke's wavy golden locks against Owen's hair that had turned grey above the ears before the poet had turned twenty-five. My purpose was legitimate: to show students, through poetry, how radically sensibilities may change once they confront historical circumstance. Yet I was aware, even as I was engaging in this dialectic, that I was not being completely fair to Brooke.

For one thing, it is incorrect to call "The Soldier" a war poem since Brooke had seen no war when he wrote it. Its original, more honest title was "The Recruit." I also knew there was something unjust in my pedagogical set-up. Poetry resents being used

Perishing Things and Strange Ghosts

in a didactic manner; it insists on its autonomy, its self-evolution, even in the case of a poem like Brooke's where the poet is using his voice to express a popular, public emotion.

Something more happened over the years I continued to teach "The Soldier." I came to appreciate its technical mastery and musicality and to forgive its content and sentimentality. I also began to wonder what accounted for my shifting taste. Wilfred Owen's anger, his cutting irony and despair, have been major influences on poetic sensibility in this century. His work has served as a touchstone for the darkness of Ted Hughes and the cynical resolve of Philip Larkin.[1] One hears echoes of the note he originally sounded behind the lines of Plath's "Daddy" and Ginsberg's "Howl." Perhaps Ginsberg's famous line, "I saw the best minds of my generation destroyed by madness, starving, hysterical, naked..." would more likely have been spoken by a survivor of the Somme than by a victim of corporate America. If there is any doubt about the connection in Ginsberg's imagination between the individual's struggle in America in the mid-fifties and the Great War, one need only look to the following passage in "Howl." Ginsberg is writing about those of his generation

> who were burned alive in their innocent flannel suits on Madison Avenue amid blasts of leaden verse and the tanked-up clatter of the iron regiments of fashion & nitroglycerine shrieks....& the mustard gas of sinister intelligent editors

It may well be that my growing acceptance of Brooke's poem was born of a growing disaffection for the eschatological darkness poetry has been stuck with since the Great War; it may indicate my wish to find something green and living beyond the wasteland.

Though Rupert Brooke's literary stock has been plummeting for the last half century, it is interesting to note that such disparate figures as D. H. Lawrence, T. S. Eliot, and Henry James took his work seriously. I remember that in high school, in the 1960's, in addition to "The Soldier," our class read Brooke's "The Great Lover" and "The Hill." But reading through Brooke's *Collected Poems*, one realizes that his best poems are those modeled after English Metaphysical poetry. It is not surprising to find among his essays a perceptive study of Andrew Marvell, and it is unfortunate that Brooke's more poignant, metaphysical poems, such as "Dust" or "The Call" are never anthologized. Still, one has to admit that much of Brooke's earlier poetry seems to be largely apprentice work — skilled, technically adept, but also derivative and uninformed by experience. The one dazzling exception is "The Fish," the poem that T. S. Eliot[2] singled out in a review published in *The Egoist,* claiming that it displayed "a really amazing felicity and command of language." One can imagine its primal vividness, its "serpentine" world, also appealing to Lawrence:

> *In a cool curving world he lies*
> *And ripples with dark ecstasies.*
> *The kind luxurious lapse and steal*
> *Shapes all his universe to feel*
> *And know and be; the clinging stream*
> *Closes his memory, glooms his dream,*
> *Who lips the roots o' the shore, and glides*
> *Superb on unreturning tides.*

Brooke's fish inhabits

> *An obscure world, a shifting world,*
> *Bulbous, or pulled to thin, or curled,*
> *Or serpentine, or diving arrows,*
> *Or serene slidings, or March narrows.*
> *There slipping wave and shore are one,*
> *And weed and mud. No ray of sun,*
> *But glow to glow fades down the deep*
> *(As dream to unknown dream in sleep)*

There is a strange blend here of visceral descriptiveness and metaphysical abstraction, carried by the Marvell-like octosyllabic couplets. This creates a dynamic tension that allows Brooke to write from inside the fish-world as well as conjecture about it from without. The heightened attention to language — for example, using nouns like "gloom" and "lips" as verbs — helps Brooke

Perishing Things and Strange Ghosts

avoid his usual emotional pit-fall: sentimentality. The poem contrasts the warm human world ("O world of lips, world of laughter") with a cold, nether world ("But there the night is close, and there/Darkness is cold and strange and bare") — an anti-world to the one Brooke typically chose to articulate.

It is that cold world that reappears in the sonnet sequence Brooke will write in 1913, titled "The South Seas." In these poems a distinct voice begins to emerge. Though these poems do not possess the rhythmic speed or exuberance of language exhibited by "The Fish," they take from that poem a detachment and objectivity that Brooke now employs in more serious and meditative poems. The sense of loss in these poems comes out of Brooke's broken affair with Ka Cox. There is a Baudelairian sadness and sense of futility in poems like "Hauntings," Mutability," or "Clouds," where the sky's shifting white masses serve as a metaphor for "the Dead" who

> *ride the calm mid-heaven, as these,*
> *In wide majestic train,*
> *And watch the moon, and the still-raging seas,*
> *And men, coming and going on the earth.*

Life's commotion has slowed down; the poet is no longer trying to console himself by latching onto traditional poetic solutions, but instead, is attempting to find words adequate to his spiritual state. These poems are authentic and quietly urgent enough to encourage one to disagree with Larkin's assessment that had Brooke lived, "there seems small likelihood that he would have found sufficient fulfillment in writing verse," or with his sarcastic conclusion that Brooke, with his political ideas and his good looks, "might have become leader of the liberal party." [3] There is something deeper going on in these sonnets. They may be regarded as preparation for the last poem Rupert Brooke would write, the one that prompted my inquiry into his work. It is a deeply moving and prophetic poem, exceptional not only within the context of Brooke's *Collected Poems*, but within the canon of Great War poetry.

It has the unintentionally apt and ironic title "Fragment," (provided, I suppose, by Brooke's friend and editor, Edward Marsh).

Corpse-making trench warfare would soon make dismemberment, or fragmentation, universally familiar. The poem, found in the notebook Brooke was using in the weeks before his death, helps formulate an answer to the question: "What if Brooke had lived to write about the war?"

FRAGMENT

I strayed about the deck, an hour, to-night
Under a cloudy moonless sky; and peeped
In at windows, watched my friends at table,
Or playing cards, or standing in the doorway,
Or coming out into the darkness. Still
No one could see me.

I would have thought of them
— Heedless, within a week of battle — in pity,
Pride in their strength and in the weight and firmness
And link'd beauty of bodies, and pity that
This gay machine of splendour'ld soon be broken,
Thought little of, pashed, scattered...

Only, always,
I could but see them — against the lamplight — pass
Like coloured shadows, thinner than filmy glass,
Slight bubbles, fainter than the wave's faint light,
That broke to phosphorous out in the night,
Perishing things and strange ghosts — soon to die
To other ghosts — this one, or that, or I.

April, 1915

The poem's sensitivity to the suffering inherent in war and its prophecy of annihilation may have originated in Brooke's witnessing the sacking of Antwerp. He was deeply affected by the sight of fleeing Belgian refugees. In his notebook, he describes "the old men mostly weeping, the women with hard drawn faces,

Perishing Things and Strange Ghosts

the children crying or asleep." He goes on to comment: "But it's a bloody thing, half the youth of Europe, blown through pain to nothingness." To use Wallace Stevens's memorable phrase, it is "the nothingness that is" which informs this final poem, whose sensibility marks a significant departure from anything else Brooke had written. The poet-speaker finds himself, not in a romantic, but in a realistic and mundane setting — walking the deck of his ship. The tone, no longer that of an exuberant recruit, is introspective and mature. The poet no longer counts himself one of those "blessed suns" of "The Soldier." He has become the outsider, a voyeur, peering in at his fellow officers. Wrapped in "darkness," he remains invisible, unrecognized. "No one could see me."

Significantly, Brooke uses the word "pity" twice in the poem; this is a direct link to the compassion we find in Wilfred Owen's work. "Pity" is the key word in Owen's terse and unforgettable preface to his poems:

> *This book is not about heroes. English poetry is not yet fit to speak of them...*
> *Above all I am not concerned with Poetry.*
> *My subject is War, and the pity of War.*
> *The Poetry is in the pity.*

In *The Great War And Modern Memory*, Fussell points out the degree to which the compassion of First World War poets was homoerotic. Brooke foregrounds this in the lines "Pride in their strength and in the weight and firmness/And link'd beauty of bodies...gay machine of splendour." But while in "The Soldier," the soon-to-be-dead poet-warrior believes that he and his comrades will live forever in the nation's memory, the speaker in "Fragment" sees the dead as "broken/thought little of, pashed, scattered..." Only one year separates "The Soldier" from this "Fragment," yet it seems as if the sensibilities of the poems belong to two different periods. Such radical shifts in consciousness were noted by several poets of the time, perhaps most memorably by Anna Akhmatova who wrote: "The 20th century began in the fall of 1914 along with the war. We grew 100 years older and it happened in an hour." For Rupert Brooke, with all his cultural baggage, that hour came a bit later, in the spring of 1915.

The sense of loss and futility that Brooke first experienced in his troubled love affair with Ka Cox and exhibited in his "South Seas" poems, is extended and amplified here as he stands, not before the dark side of Venus, but before the ultimate destructive agent, Mars. And yet, though Brooke has grown out of the youthful optimism and inexperience evidenced in his earliest poems, he has not completely relinquished his former sense of affirmation, or his former style, both of which move like shadows behind the lines of this poem. The man who catalogued all that he cherished in "The Great Lover," who wrote with such intuitiveness about "The Fish," who once said, "There are only three good things in the world — one is to read poetry, another is to write poetry, and best of all is to live poetry" — that upholder of life stands behind the loss in this poem and provides its unique tone. It is as if some hedonist with a flute had been lowered into Hell and asked to bring back a report.

Brooke did not fail. If before this time the only ghosts he knew were green, Platonic ones found in his volumes of Metaphysical poetry, they now have names and faces, attached, no doubt, to his Cambridge graduation photo, or to the men on board his ship who will be killed at Gallipoli. These are the poem's "strange ghosts" — strange because they still have flesh, walk and speak. But Brooke has seen them in the underworld. Descending into the realm of "shadows" and "phosphorous," he has seen his double (the "I" of the last line) — a sign, Borges tells us, not only of the perceiver's own impending death, but also of his prophetic power.[4] The "perishing things" of the poem are all those delights of Brooke's former world that he realizes will be "blown through pain to nothingness." Yet there is no rage in this descent; it is reported with a gentle touch: "filmy glass," "bubbles," "coloured shadows," "faint light," all conjure the tenuousness of existence.

In this last poem, abandoning his place of privilege, his imaginary English garden, Brooke reaches out to touch suffering humanity. He intuits that the desolation created by the Great War will turn the self, the "I", into a phantom. His "perishing things" extend to include those cherished beliefs that Owen condemned as "false creeds." The tragedy of Rupert Brooke is that, had he lived, his poetic elegance and wit — brought to bear upon the

Perishing Things and Strange Ghosts

unfolding nightmare — would have produced a poetry in voice less angry than Owen's and in technique less muscular, yet no less mordant and disquieting.

NOTES

[1] See Hughes' poem "Wilfred Owen's Photographs" and Larkin's review/essay "The War Poet."

[2] As a point of interest, compare Brooke's "The Soldier" to T.S. Eliot's commemorative World War II poem, "To The Indians Who Died In Africa," which contains the lines

> *Where a man dies bravely*
> *At one with his destiny, that soil is his.*
> *Let his village remember.*

[3] See Larkin's review/essay "The Apollo Bit" in his collection *Required Writing*.

[4] See "The Double" in Jorge Luis Borges' *The Book Of Imaginary Beings*.

ARE WE NOT MEN ? H.G. WELLS' *THE ISLAND OF DOCTOR MOREAU*

This year marks the centenary of the publication of H.G. Wells' novel *The Island of Doctor Moreau*. I am probably representative of my generation when I report that my first encounter with the novel was through a black and white film I watched on television — *The Island of Lost Souls*, starring Charles Laughton. To this day I recall the scene of the Beast Folk sitting around a fire chanting the Law: "Not to go on all-Fours; *that* is the Law. Are we not Men?" There were close-ups of their half-lit faces, some with pig noses, others with oxen lips: images striking enough to stay in my memory for thirty-five years, but not as striking as the novel I would read as an adult. Then I would understand that it was not the Beast Folk who were horrific, but their human creator, Doctor Moreau; and what Moreau thought was as terrifying as what he did.

The popular view of H.G. Wells is that he was a science fiction writer and pseudo social critic. But before he began writing pamphlets and didactic novels (what one of his contemporary critics called "sociological cocktails"), he was a formidable mythmaker, a creator of dark and perplexing romances. Of Wells' famous early novels — *The Time Machine, The Invisible Man, The War of The Worlds* — *The Island of Doctor Moreau* is the only one which received near unanimous condemnation from the initial

Are We Not Men?

reviewers. "Blasphemous," "sacrilegious," and "indecent," are the pejoratives one reads in these reviews. Wells himself termed the work a "theological grotesque." The book was stimulated in part by the philosophical ramifications of Darwin's theories; it uncannily foreshadowed the insights and influences of Nietszche and Freud, and foretold the darkest historical events of our century. Of Wells' five major romances, it is the least widely read and taught — a confirmation, perhaps, of its discomforting truths.

For those who have not read the book, here is a brief outline: The narrator is Edward Prendick. Like Wells himself, he is a liberal humanist who has studied science. Prendick is shipwrecked, rescued and taken to an island. There he discovers that his host, Doctor Moreau, is transporting animals to the island so that he can conduct hideous experiments on them. Through vivisection, plastic surgery and behavioural modification, Moreau is attempting to transform these animals into humans. He has partially succeeded. Some of the Beast Folk, however, keep reverting back to their old ways and Moreau is eventually killed by one of his own creations. After that, the Beast Folk regress and destroy one another. Prendick manages to escape the island and make his way back to England where he tells his tale. He is considered insane but harmless and lives out his last days in voluntary isolation, unable to bear the sight of his fellow human beings.

On the most obvious level the book is a Swiftian satire following in the wake of Darwin's findings. Man has usurped the role of God, and the power of science has overtaken that of religion. The Beast Folk are conditioned to think of Moreau as a deity. He has attempted to civilize them and when they disobey him they are sent back to the laboratory, called The House of Pain. They are taught to meet regularly and ordered to chant The Law in words that are a parody of the Ten Commandments. This is Wells' "theological grotesque." But *The Island of Doctor Moreau* is one of those books that, in the aftermath of historical events, can be read as a prophecy; it is a work which says more than its author intended.

Moreau's island is a totalitarian state and Moreau himself, a fascmst; his values seem based upon the Nazi perversion of Nietzsche's *Übermensch* philosophy. We do not know whether

Wells read Nietzsche or not. If so, he was one of the first Englishmen to do so since the earliest translations appeared in 1895, the year he wrote his book. Even if Wells had not read the author of *The Will To Power*, it is not surprising that he should intuit some of the German thinker's ideas as well as the ways they might be misconstrued. Authors do not possess crystal balls; whatever is prophetic in their work is built upon the acute observations they make of their own time and in this book, Wells, in part, is presenting a picture of late nineteenth century colonialism. Moreau is described as "the white-haired man," "powerfully built" possessing "an expression of pugnacious resolution." At one point he explains how he created his first man, transforming a gorilla into "a fair specimen of the Negroid type." Even Prendick, the English humanist, feels no need to disguise his racism. He tells us that one of the Beast People has a face "like the coarser Hebrew type — his voice a harsh bleat, his nether extremities Satanic."

Through the character of Moreau, Wells has provided us with an astonishingly exact and detailed analysis of the fascistic personality. Moreau detests the animals he has transported to the island for their creatureliness. He thinks of them as weak. He despises their very essence and wishes to take hold of it: "Their intelligence is often oddly low," he tells Prendick, "with unaccountable blank ends, unexpected gaps. And least satisfactory of all is something that I cannot touch, somewhere — I cannot determine where — in the seat of the emotions." Just as the Nazis wished to purify those whom they considered beneath them, so Moreau wishes to do the same with his beasts. In words that could have issued from the mouth of Mengele, he states, "I will conquer yet. Each time I dip a living creature into a bath of pain, I say, This time I will burn out the animal..."

For Moreau, pain is "a useless thing, needless." He firmly believes he is superior to those who live in the realm of sensations. As he tells Prendick, "Pain and pleasure — they are for us, so long as we wriggle in the dust..." Man's role is to supersede pain, to have it count for next to nothing so that he can ready himself for the extreme tasks ahead. The irony is that in denying his own flesh, his own creatureliness, Moreau has made himself not more human, but inhuman. Sadistic, driven, he is the book's true monster. From the laboratory located next to his guest room, Prendick, the book's "witness," hears the unceasing "crying of the puma" as it is being operated on and says prophetically "It was as if all the pain in the world had found a voice."

And yet it would be too easy to dismiss Moreau as merely a fanatical Nazi. The story's ultimate meaning is far more unsettling. For though Moreau is fascistic, he is not an ideologue. He belongs to no political party or religious sect. He is first and foremost an experimental scientist, yet it is difficult to find any rationale for his experiments. He is most comparable to his heirs — those S.S. doctors in the concentration camps who performed bizarre and needless experiments on innocent victims. Prendick rightly calls Moreau "irresponsible" and states, "His curiosity, his mad, aimless investigations, drove him on." Moreau, he believes, can never be forgiven because he has no "motive."

Wells' scientist friends objected strongly to *The Island Of Doctor Moreau,* complaining that unlike his other books, this one presented a negative picture of their profession. They were right, of course. But the book is more than a critique of science: Moreau is that part of Western man that is rigid, obsessive, mistrustful of Nature, lacking in love and in meaningfulness. It would be too convenient to call him "a mad scientist." If he is insane, it is an insanity based on rationalism taken to its extreme in a decadent, non-spiritual age. He is highly sophisticated technological man lacking a humanistic foundation or horizon. As such, there is a portion of him in all of us, and the complete annihilation of life on his island (a metaphor for our world) is a possibility we also face.

Wells expands the limits of these questions regarding our inhumanity through his use of Moreau's victims, the Beast People. Animals have made their appearance in literature in many ways. One of the more common is the beast fable. In these we meet characters with animal bodies but human consciousness. If there is a protagonist who has spent time in this community of animals (for example, Tarzan) he or she is often heroic. In our century, the beast fable is more often a satire of human society (for example, George Orwell's *Animal Farm*). But *The Island of Doctor Moreau* is not strictly a beast fable for the descriptions are not, as in traditional beast fables, fantastic, but realistic. Such bizarre scenes rendered realistically lead us forward to Kafka's *Metamorphosis*. What Wells is able to achieve in his book is a sustained blurring of the distinction between man and animal, between the human and non-human. The reader experiences this through the narrator's confusion: at the beginning of the novel Prendick thinks that the hideous creatures he sees on the island are misshapen men; later he supposes they are men who have been surgically changed into animals; we are half way through the story before he comprehends that he is looking at humanized beasts.

It is understandable why those initial reviewers of the book felt indignant when reading it; throughout the novel we have a strong sense of the repulsive, the horrific, the unclean. But it is not the ugliness of the Beast People that gives us this impression. The deeper cause is ontological. Consider the following two passages from Chapter 12, where Prendick comes to the lair of the Beast Folk:

> Then something cold touched my hand. I started violently, and saw close to me a dim pinkish thing, looking more like a flayed child than anything else in the world. The creature had exactly the mild but repulsive features of a sloth, the same low forehead and slow gestures.
>
> He put out a strangely distorted talon, and gripped my fingers. The thing was almost like the hoof of a deer produced into claws. I could have yelled with surprise and pain. His face came forward and I saw with a quivering disgust that it was like the face of neither man nor beast ...

To Wells' contemporaries these descriptions would have suggested the Darwinian animalization of man. But for us, this blurred distinction points to the moral dilemma posed by the inhumanity of Moreau and to that question which the Beast People insistently ask themselves throughout the book: *Are we not Men?* We can re-phrase this in more general and non-gender terms as, *What is a human being?* Books resonate uncannily into the future and I cannot help but read a profound link between the question posed by the Beasts and the title of Primo Levi's first book, *If This Is*

Man. In the concentration camps, inmates were referred to as vermin and lice; they were treated like non-humans. And those who pointed children the way to the gas chambers — were they beasts? Perhaps we have not yet found an adequate term for them. It is apparent that this question — *What is a human being?* has become pervasive. We see it repeated in popular film though here, under the impact of technology, the line is most often blurred not between humans and animals, but between humans and forms of artificial intelligence. Is the replicant Roy in the film *Bladerunner* more or less human than his assassin? Is Edward Scissorhands more or less human than the suburbanites with whom he lives for a brief time? In both films our hearts go out to the non-human characters.

Though humans are often despicable in *The Island of Doctor Moreau*, Wells does not, like his contemporaries Rudyard Kipling (*The Jungle Book*) and Edgar Rice Burroughs (*Tarzan of the Apes*), romanticize Nature. There is no Mowgli or Tarzan; no naive Wild Child; no innocent Casper Hauser. Nature is not nurturing but dark, and it will be darker if man meddles unwisely. Since man has meddled we feel some sympathy for the animals. Watching them degenerate from their near-human status, Prendick observes: "Before, they had been beasts... happy as living things may be. Now they stumbled in the shackles of humanity... wretched in themselves." He reports that as the Beast Folk became more like animals, they "felt ashamed of themselves." Though shame is thought to be a human characteristic, it is something Doctor Moreau never feels.

The last chapter, "The Man Alone," is most prescient. Prendick has survived two major catastrophes: the story's opening shipwreck (grisly scenes of violence and proposed cannibalism foreshadow the horrors to be enacted later) and the annihilation of life on Moreau's island. He has met the human monster in the form of an accomplished surgeon. Returning to England, Prendick bears all the traits of a Survivor: fearful, alienated, he lives half in the present, half in the painful past; eventually, he stops telling his tale so that people will stop thinking he is deranged. He suffers from depression, anxiety and a sense that existence is absurd. His experience of London is hallucinogenic. Urbanites transform into animals: prowling women "mew" after him; "weary paleworkers" are suddenly "wounded deer dripping blood;" a preacher in a church turns into the Ape Man gibbering fatuous nonsense, what the Beast Folk called 'big thinks.' There is a death pall over the city: "Particularly nauseous were the blank expressionless faces of people in trains and omnibuses; they seemed no more my fellow-creatures than dead bodies would be."

This is the urban inferno that will reappear again and again in modern literature. In this ghoulish, concrete landscape, Prendick claims that he cannot find "a reasonable soul" and questions his own rationality when he is amongst people. For rationalism has led to the "scientific" horrors he has witnessed. Nevertheless, as a true modern he must in the end side with science and the possibility of reason. He becomes reclusive, applying himself solely to the study of chemistry and astronomy — pure sciences that require no human interaction. He believes that it is in those fields, "in the vast and eternal laws of matter," that hope for mankind lies. It is not to be found, he is sure, "in the daily cares and sins and troubles of men." We are left with a distraught, intelligent witness, who shuns human society; one who is considered insane, yet bears the truth.

So begins the twentieth century.

WHAT THE LINE WAS AFTER: JOSEPH BRODSKY'S *ON GRIEF AND REASON*

With the death of Joseph Brodsky earlier this year, twentieth century Russian poetry comes full circle. It began with Mandelstam, Akhmatova, Tsvetaeva and Pasternak — brilliant poets who created their early works in the Soviet Union's relatively benign pre-Stalinist era. Their later sufferings during the reign of terror would include, imprisonment and death, ostracism, suicide, and censorship.

Brodsky's career went in the opposite direction. Arrested at the age of 23 for being a "social parasite" (writing poetry without the proper credentials), he served two years hard labour in Russia's wastelands. In 1972 the Soviets expelled him, unwittingly presenting the West with a priceless gift. In the U.S., Brodsky began to write in English, recited his poetry for large audiences, and published his essays in *The New Yorker*. He lived to witness the demise of the regime that had persecuted him and died close to the end of the century in Brooklyn Heights, a free man.

On Grief and Reason, his second essay collection, appeared a few weeks before his death. It contains twenty-one pieces, some of them occasional addresses for conferences or university commencements. While these lighter, entertaining pieces are often of interest, the book's importance lies with its eight major essays.

Some readers may find them overly demanding because for Brodsky, prose was the continuation of his poetry by other means. The Polish poet Stanislaw Baranczak correctly observed that Brodsky's essays — reminiscences, homages and close readings of poems — are the prose equivalents of the elegy, the hymn of praise, and the ars poetica. But this only partly explains their demanding nature.

The other reason is that though Brodsky wrote some of his later work in English, though he claimed to identify with Donne and Auden, he was first and foremost a Russian poet. Consequently, when he writes in English his feeling for language remains Russian, and as he himself observes, "English is an analytical language," while "Russian is highly inflected." This conflict may account for his occasional convoluted sentences, verbosity, and misuse of colloquialisms, while his sporadic chattiness may be an attempt to mask his insecurity with English. Yet even without these weaknesses, the English speaking reader would find Brodsky demanding since his style is outside the realm of the traditional English essay. His prose is aphoristic, witty, metaphysical in intent, and erratic in thought rather than strictly logical. Even so, it is worth reading. Every style has its traps and while Brodsky's is at times frustrating, its leaps often take us to intellectual frontiers where few writers would be willing to travel.

Not only does one's semantic ground have its own laws, its own directional imperative, it also tends to determine one's true poetic progenitors. Brodsky's first book of essays, *Less Than One*, contains a piece entitled "A Poet and Prose." It is a consideration of the essays of Marina Tsvetaeva. It is also the closest Brodsky ever came to describing his own approach to writing prose.

He tells us that Tsvetaeva's reader is "dealing not with a linear (analytic) development but with a crystalline (synthesizing) growth of thought." He describes her style, as well as her contemporary Mandelstam's, as characterized by "linguistic and metaphorical density," and "linguistic oversaturation." He notes that Tsvetaeva's work expresses "her constant endeavour to raise the pitch a note higher, an idea higher." Readers of Mandelstam and Tsvetaeva will recognize this expansive, risk-taking quality in Brodsky's essays and concur that there is nothing like it in traditional English criticism. Its salutary effect on Western po-

What The Line Was After

etry was noted by Seamus Heaney in his essay, "The Government Of The Tongue" where he compared T. S. Eliot's reading of Dante as a didactic, theological poet, to Mandelstam's liberating view of Dante as (in Heaney's words) "the epitome of chemical suddenness ... the sponsor of impulse and instinct."

Three of the major essays in this book are close readings of poets: "On Grief And Reason"(Frost), "Ninety Years Later"(Rilke), and "Wooing The Inanimate" (Hardy). In the title piece Brodsky examines the language in Robert Frost's poem "Home Burial" which deals with the conflict between a husband and wife who have recently lost a child. This reading is an elaboration of Lionel Trilling's description of Frost as "a terrifying poet." Brodsky reveals Frost's astonishing degree of detachment, even in dealing with so emotional a subject as the loss of a child. He assures us that Frost's autobiography — the truth of his "dark" character — is in his use of language, not in the mere facts of his life. The poem is an argument, not so much between a wife and husband (though even on that level it reveals more than a sociology or self-help text) but between grief and reason, passion and intellect, Dionysus and Apollo — what Brodsky refers to as "poetry's indelible ink."

In the piece on Rilke's "Orpheus. Eurydice. Hermes," Brodsky writes intriguingly about mythology in regards to primal man's acquaintance with caves, burial sites and the netherworld. His comments on the origins of "verse" (from the Latin *versus*, which means "turn") force us to think more deeply about the Orpheus myth in which a poet's turning is an error that costs him a loved one. His detailed sensitivity to this beautiful and heartbreaking poem, animates and subtly accentuates its effectiveness.

Brodsky reads each poem with his eyes, ears, and intellect, attentive to the poem's imagery, musicality and thought. Each is a full reading, "saturated," to use his term, though never pretending to be definitive or final. He makes a point of emphasizing the "dash, not a period" that Frost employs at the conclusion of "Home Burial", and the missing period after the god's name in Rilke's title "Orpheus. Eurydice. Hermes" because for Brodsky, "what has been uttered is never the end but the edge of speech, which — owing to the existence of time — is followed by something. And what follows is always more interesting than what has been said." Hence, Brodsky's prose, characterized by speed and desire, rarely feels contained; it is always groping after more: the next striking image, witticism, revelation. He is constantly attempting to raise the metaphysical ante.

It is not surprising that in the essays of a linguistically acrobatic author like Brodsky, language itself emerges as a protagonist. Not that Brodsky is in any way a deconstructionist, who thinks literature is self-referential and solipsistic. His starting points are the Hebraic notion that God is a Name, and the statement of John's Gospel, "In the beginning was the Word." As he states in "Ninety Years Later" — "Mimesis precedes genesis" — which I take to mean that poetry, or inventive language, defines being or existence. The question of language and existence is most fully extended in his lengthy essay "Wooing The Inanimate," a consideration of Thomas Hardy's poetry.

Brodsky provides an expert reading of five Hardy poems, as he tries to explain the poet's contemporaneity. This has to do, he says, with Hardy's voice of detachment, his "audial neutrality" which was a result of his "appetite for the infinite and the inanimate." Hardy's particular genius was in cutting back on Victorian sentimentality. To do this he looked to the world of things, of inanimate matter. In this sense he was being prescient, since, as Brodsky states, "the truth about the world" is "nonhuman." Hardy went after the inanimate "for its diction." Language, as Brodsky understands it, is also a thing, a part of the inanimate world; in fact it is "the inanimate's first line of information about itself, released to the animate."

This is an interesting observation and allows us to link Hardy to contemporary European anti-poetry, to the detached voice, for instance, of Zbignieff Herbert as contemplates the coldness of a pebble. To help us understand the meaning of Hardy's insights, Brodsky connects them to Schopenhauer's notion of The Immanent Will, "the nonrational force and its blind, striving power operating in the world." We may also think of Camus' "indifference of the universe," for Brodsky uses the term "existential truth" when praising Hardy's relevance to our age.

The truth that Hardy discovers, however, is not his doing alone. He must share that with language, and it is here, at the point where Brodsky invests language with a presence all its own

What The Line Was After

that we may have trouble accepting his argument. Brodsky believes "language is capable of arrangements that reduce a human being to, at best, the function of a scribe ... that utilize a human being, not the other way around." Discussing the effectiveness of a poem, he states: "I am far from suggesting that this is what Thomas Hardy was after in this line. Rather, it was what the line was after in Thomas Hardy."

What does Brodsky accomplish by regarding language as a separate entity? It is common to regard language as a tool, forgetting that it is capable of mutation and transformation. Brodsky likens it to a changeable yet essential element, comparable to "our own cellular mixture." This allows him to release it from the mundane, to invest it with the power — and perhaps mystery — it possesses. It also enables him to limit the egocentricity of the poet, making him a servant of language, not a Romantic demigod. After a poet dies, the Muse "finds herself another mouthpiece in the next generation." This theme of humility runs throughout these essays. In his reminiscence of Stephen Spender, for instance, Brodsky writes: "If you are not born with some organic disorder, poetry — writing it as well as reading it — will teach you humility... The dead alone will set you straight fast."

But if such a view of language demotes the poet, it certainly elevates poetry itself, perhaps to the level of a quasi-religion. It is difficult to accept the idea that language is an entity unto itself, because it is so dependent on its relationship to us, as readers, writers, and speakers. We are responsible for its shifts and permutations. In the beginning may have been the Word, but it required a human to utter it. And was that human merely a "scribe" taking down what was dictated, or did he or she modify, edit, perhaps even censor?

This essay on Hardy (actually, it is a lecture) runs sixty-four pages and one wonders if this length is necessary. It is fair to say that Brodsky's previous collection, *Less Than One*, is a tighter book with its superbly condensed observations on the poets Cavafy, Montale, Akhmatova, and Mandelstam. In those essays, Brodsky did the hard work for the reader while in *On Grief And Reason* he is more apt to take one through the various steps of his enquiry and conclusions. Still, there are segments in these lengthy essays where he displays his laser-like capacity to pinpoint a poet's essential qualities. The following are his comments on Rilke: "He is a poet of isolation, and isolating the subject is his forte. Give him a subject and he will turn it into an object, take it out of its context, and go for its core, inhabiting it with his extraordinary erudition, intuitions, and instinct for allusion. The net result is that the subject becomes his, colonized by the intensity of his attention and imagination."

One may ask whether explicating a poem is self-defeating, like explaining a joke. Unlike a joke, though, poetry depends on recognition — knowing again — and to re-read a poem after it has been explicated augments our enjoyment of it. It also leads us off onto our own tangential interpretations. In his essay on Rilke, Brodsky states that "translation is the father of civilization," and it may be that all of his close reading is an attempt to civilize his audience by translating poetry into terms that might make us more sensitive to language, more aware of our imaginative selves. The audience for poetry has become small; Brodsky estimates it throughout the ages at 1% of the population, but guesses (based on statistics of poetry book sales) that in North America it is now .001% of the population. It is possible for human beings to lose certain faculties: How many of us can sit through a drama by Shakespeare? How many can re-read an Emily Dickinson poem until the layers begin to reveal themselves? This has to do with our lack of concentration, insensitivity to the nuances of language, incapacity to respond to allusions and references, whether they be biblical, mythical, or literary.

Brodsky has a belief in poetry's ability to cure civilizations of violence, to unite us with the past, as well as to free us from personal neuroses. In his less intellectual pieces, he has chosen to act as a promoter of poetry. In an address to the Library of Congress, he proposes that the U. S. government print 2.5 million copies of poetry books and sell them for two dollars a piece. "Poetry," he says, "should be as ubiquitous as gas stations." He rails about "a tremendous cultural backslide" and predicts that a man "unable to articulate, to express himself adequately ... is bound to act violently, extending his vocabulary with a weapon where there should have been an adjective." In his address to the Turin book fair, he tells his listeners that they should read poetry, as opposed to novels, if they wish to develop sound taste in lit-

What The Line Was After

erature, since poetry, precise, laconic and epigrammatic, "offers the highest possible standards for any linguistic operation."

Not all of *On Grief and Reason* is concerned with the subject of poetry. Some pieces, continuing in the vein of "In a Room and a Half" from Brodsky's earlier collection, are autobiographical. The most charming of these is "Spoils of War," in which Brodsky remembers the pleasant intrusion of Western objects and sounds into post-war Russia. American films, canned meat, portable radios — all are scrutinized as emblems of a world Brodsky and his peers long to inhabit. His walk through "some grimy industrial outskirt of Leningrad" and suddenly hearing out of an open window the voice of Ella Fitzgerald singing "A-tisket, A-tasket," is most evocative.

In two of his finest essays, Brodsky is able to penetrate the curtain of time by attaching himself to classical figures. In "Homage to Marcus Aurelius" his subject is ethics; in "Letter to Horace," poetry.

The essay on the Emperor Aurelius is the most perfectly written in the book. This may be because Brodsky has chosen a voice unlike his own. The style of Aurelius' *Meditations,* slow, brooding, melancholic, seems to have had a stabilizing effect on Brodsky's prose. Describing the goodness of Marcus, Brodsky writes:

"He has surprisingly little blood on his hands. He would rather pardon than punish those who rebelled against him; those who fought him, he would rather subdue than destroy. The laws he made benefitted the most powerless: widows, slaves... he didn't like *circenze* that much and when he had to attend a show, he is reported to have read or written or been briefed during the performance. It was he, however, who introduced to the Roman Circus the safety net for acrobats."

According to Brodsky, antiquity is an arbitrary concept we have created, not only to falsely organize the past, but to distance ourselves from it. So doing, we feel superior. It is true that most of us harbour an evolutionary notion of history that could be illustrated by an upward moving line labelled *progress.* "And what," Brodsky asks, "if the very notion of such evolution is a lie?" The purpose of studying Aurelius' *Meditations* is to realize that there is something absolute about fairness and goodness; Aurelius would be considered a moral man today (certainly a more impressive ruler than the banal ones we elect). "Ethics," Brodsky says, "is the criterion of the present ... it turns every yesterday and tomorrow into now."

Poetry does the same. In his "Letter to Horace" (an inventive example of what Auden called "breaking bread with the dead"), Brodsky writes to the shade of the Roman poet, confident he can communicate with him. Counting the years between them, Brodsky asks, "Two thousand years — of what? By whose count, Flaccus? Certainly not in terms of metrics. Tetrameters are tetrameters, no matter when and no matter where. Be they in Greek, Latin, Russian, English ... When it comes to collapsing time, our trade, I am afraid, beats history..."

Not only does poetry collapse time, it also preserves the vibrancy of experience. Therefore, it is not strange for Brodsky to confess to Horace that he feels the dead poet's presence more than that of a remembered love affair: "To me, your reality is practically greater than that of my private memory." Since life is for the most part disjointed and amorphous, poetry, which Brodsky claims "restructures time," has the ability to intensify or focus it in such a way as to make it memorable. A poem is not "a metaphor for reality but a reality itself."

And if we were to enquire why reality aspires to poetry, Brodsky would answer, "*Cupidas.* Appetite. Desire." In the short but brilliant essay, "Altra Ego," Brodsky muses on the root of lyrical poetry. After questioning the romantic and relatively recent notion of the poet as a Don Juan figure, after condemning literary biographies (the "bad-mouthing of poets") whose purpose is to belittle poetry's authority, he states the seriousness of the poet's romantic quest: "Love is a metaphysical affair whose goal is either accomplishing or liberating one's soul." The loved one is a visage of the poet's own psyche. As for the poem, it is "an act of love, not so much of an author for his subject as of language for a piece of reality." According to Brodsky, there are two things happening simultaneously in the composing of lyric poetry: the poet longing for his love and the Muse (language) longing to be articulated.

Metamorphosis emerges as Brodsky's grand motif: the mutability and transferability of language, love, personalities. Brodsky liked to quote Tsvetaeva's aphorism, "Reading is complicity in the creative process," and believed that when one reads an author, one actually becomes him or her. That is why he asks his audience in "On Grief and Reason," "Would you like to become Robert Frost?" That is why he can see himself conversing with Horace in the netherworld, even if it is only by tapping poetic rhythms. He believed in a poet's afterlife. Reading him, we are it.

ORPHEUS DESCENDING: TOMAS TRANSTRÖMER'S *FOR THE LIVING AND THE DEAD*

The publication of a complete and recent collection of Tomas Tranströmer's poems, in English translation, is a just cause for celebration. One of the most significant poets in the Western World, Tranströmer gained fame in his native Sweden in 1954 with his first collection, *17 Poems*. In 1972, two book-length selections of his work appeared in English: Robert Bly's *Night Vision* and May Swenson's *Windows and Stones*. Since then his work has been known and admired by readers in North America and Great Britain.

Tranströmer's poetry achieves its tension through the interplay of what seem to be opposing worlds. As the title of this collection suggests, we reside with both the living and the dead. But theirs are not isolated realms whose borders are clearly demarcated: their tendency to shift, to invade each other's space, accounts for Transtromer's ironic, and, at times, reconciliatory tone.

In many of these poems, Tranströmer is Orpheus descending: "A woods in May. Here spooks my whole life," or "I am a mummy who rests in the woods' blue coffin," or "They want to say something, the dead...I'll hurry through the streets as if I'm one of them." The dead nourish Tranströmer; they lead him to states of poetic illumination, regardless of whether they float up from his

Orpheus Descending

personal past, like his murdered Second World War sea captain, or rise, like Beethoven, or the woman in a nineteenth century portrait, out of our general historical past. In fact, in these poems the personal, historical and social intermingle, providing the wide range, the many-layered quality of Tranströmer's poetry. Ultimately, the dead are both separate from us, in time past, and part of our present subconscious. Furthermore, they are potently active below much of our everyday existence:

> *We see everything and nothing, but we're*
> *straight up as periscopes controlled by*
> *the underworld's shadowy crew.*

Of course, this interplay between the worlds of the dead and the living is by no means a new one. Dramatists seem particularly disposed toward it — Ibsen, Strindberg, Beckett — and one might fault Tranströmer for presenting a world that is too blatantly dichotomous, too strictly divided between the appearance of reality and the subconscious, too psychological.

Though Tranströmer is by profession a psychologist, he is above all a poet, and the lines I have quoted above achieve poetic power, not only from the inventive submarine image, but also from the wit — "everything and nothing" — from the sarcasm behind "straight up" (rigid, righteous), and from the condemnation that we are nothing more than tools. Unlike so many contemporary poets whose visions are by and large solipsistic, Tranströmer is not content to allow the invisible, potent world to remain private. What gives his poetry weight is its tendency to move from the social — "We who live are nails hammered down into society" — toward scorn and prophecy:

> *How I loathe the expression 'a hundred per cent'!*
> *Those who cannot see anything except from the front...*
> *those who never open the wrong door and get a glimpse of the*
> *Unidentified —*
> *go past them!*

Scorn is rarely expressed in contemporary poetry, largely because there is nothing less authentic to our ears than a prophet railing on a mountaintop. Rather than preaching from a height, Tranströmer is more likely to be walking through the labyrinth of a forest or city, open to discovery. When he voices scorn, it will be alongside desperation and compassion. Note the short and brilliant "Epigram":

> *Capitalism's buildings, the hives of the killer-bees, honey for the few.*
> *There he served. But in a dark tunnel he spread his wings and flew when no one was looking. He had to live his life again.*

There are few living poets who can achieve so much in three lines: the greed and aggressiveness of capitalism, the secret flight of the stifled individual, the insistence erupting from the verb "had."

Surprisingly, Tranströmer is closest, stylistically, not to any north European, but to the Mediterranean poet, Yehuda Amichai. In his introduction to Amichai's collection *Amen*, Ted Hughes states: "Each poem is like a telephone switchboard — the images operate lightning confrontations between waiting realities..." And Tranströmer, characterizing his own work, has said: "My poems are meeting places. Their intent is to make a sudden connection between aspects of reality..." Both poets take in a flood of seemingly disparate images, conveyed by a voice modulating between surprise, irony, and pathos; this is an extremely effective device to capture the fragmentation and randomness of contemporary experience, and provides the poetry with its aura of authenticity. Paradoxically, what first appears as random ends as wisdom, for in both poets' work images are drawn together, synthesized by a powerful central intelligence, by an imagination that sees into the underlying associations of the apparent disparities.

In sensibility, Tranströmer rests somewhere between the more persistent amorousness of Amichai and the stoical terseness of the East European poets. He is more psychological and darker than Amichai, yet neither Milosz, Herbert, nor Popa would write a poem as romantic as Tranströmer's "Nightingale in Badelunda," or give us lines like "This morning my darling drove away the evil spirits ... her nakedness made the demons fly." In "Madrigal," Tranströmer writes: "I inherited a dark wood but today I am going into another wood, the bright one...."

There is another important difference between Tranströmer's existential quest and that of the Eastern European poets who have had such a powerful influence on poetry in the latter part of this century. Tranströmer is less severe and less pessimistic, though it must be stressed that his affirmation is hard-won. His quest to comprehend the perplexity of man is mirrored in his notion of human growth as a process without end. As the angel tells him in the poem "Romanesque Arches," "You will never be finished, and that's the way it should be." This process of *becoming* is reflected in the actual workings of his poems. At their best, they involve the reader in an awakening of those subconscious realities — what Tranströmer calls, the "Unidentified," "Terra Incognita" — that have been pushed aside, that are vague and slumbering. Bringing them to life is curative. And conclusions are always tentative, acknowledging the open-endedness of existence.

Like other foreign poets whose language is plainspoken and whose tone is informal — one thinks here of Cavafy, Mirsolav Holub, the late Montale — Tranströmer translates well into English. Far better, say, than Joseph Brodsky or Marina Tsvetaeva, whose poetry is grammatically more compressed, linguistically denser. To understand this from our side of the language border, imagine translating Gerard Manley Hopkins or Hart Crane, *out of* English. On the other hand, conversational poets like Walt Whitman or William Carlos Williams do well in Polish or Cantonese.

That Tranströmer translates well, in no way depreciates Don Coles' accomplishment. We are fortunate that Coles, one of Canada's finest poets, lived in Sweden for a number of years and is fluent in the language. Unlike other translators of Tranströmer, he has not had to resort to literal versions provided by an expert in Swedish. This, I suppose, is what gives his translations their immediacy and directness. Coles has vividly conveyed Transtromer's unusual and unexpected imagery. He has given us living approximations of the originals that are fluid, resonant, and most importantly, that recreate the subtly shifting frequencies of Tranströmer's tone.

Kenneth Sherman

BuschekBooks has provided us with a bilingual edition — always preferable with translations of poetry — that includes a heartfelt introduction by Coles, who wisely chose to include the reprint of a short piece from 1977, in which Tranströmer describes the possibilities for modern poetry and characterizes his poetic makings. Each of the seventeen poems in this collection is an unqualified success. Aside from short gems like "Epigram" (quoted above), there are four major poems: "Indoors is Endless," "Streets In Shanghai," "Vermeer," and "Yellowjacket." Of these, I find "Vermeer" the most exceptional; its energy arises from the tension between the crass and noisy world of money, war, and madness, and the quiet world of the master's paintings where the commotion has been stilled by art. The poem examines the nature of the barrier between these worlds, or "the wall" as Tranströmer calls it, and ends with a stanza on "the void...emptiness," where the poet reaffirms his humanism by transforming a potentially dark perspective into *possibility*:

> *And emptiness turns its face to us*
> *and whispers*
> *"I am not empty, I am open."*

# III

CRACKPOT : A LURIANIC MYTH

Into how many pieces does one break and still bother to count the pieces?

Crackpot — an intriguing title. Hoda, the novel's central character, is physically a cracked pot, a prostitute or, as she comically calls herself, a "Sexual Worker." Then there is her blind father, Danile, who is also referred to as a "crackpot." He is a Shlemiel figure. Hoda says, "There was something in Daddy that acquiesced in not knowing." His innocence and näiveté make him something of a fool, yet that same childlike quality provides him with a clear perception of thoughts and issues. He is unable or unwilling to see much of the hardcore reality around him; yet his cronies point out: "There was something of holiness about him ... his questions were not the questions of a fool."

Aside from puns and character implications, "crackpot" refers directly to the novel's epigraph:

> *He stored the Divine Light in a Vessel, but the Vessel, unable to contain Holy Radiance, burst, and its shards, permeated with sparks of the Divine, scattered through the Universe.*

This is from Ari's Kabbalistic legend of creation. Ari was Ashkenazi Reb Isaac, also known as Isaac Luria (1534-1572), a

Jewish mystic born in Jerusalem who developed a significant strain of Kabbalistic theosophy. Wiseman is not employing some esoteric bit of religious occult. In his study *Major Trends in Jewish Mysticism*, the Kabbalistic scholar Gershom Scholem points out that the Lurianic myth is a form of mysticism "which has exerted by far the greatest influence in Jewish history and which for centuries stood out in the popular mind as bearer of the final and deepest truth in Jewish thought." As evidence of this, the name of one of its major components, *Tikkun*, is now the name of a leading intellectual magazine in the U.S.

I do not wish to suggest that one can place the system of Lurianic myth over *Crackpot* and come out with a perfect fit. A novel has to have some edges hanging out, some mysterious inner pockets that the reader can delve into. But an understanding of the Lurianic myth will help us to better understand the novel's major progression.

The Lurianic Kabbalah constituted a direct response to the Jews' expulsion from Spain, and is relevant to contemporary questions raised by the Holocaust. Luria's Kabbalistic work contains a creation myth that is divided into three major experiences: *Tsimtsum*, the self-limitation or exile of God; *Shevirah*, the breaking of the vessels; *Tikkun*, the harmonious correction and mending of the flaw.

Tsimtsum, the first experience, is a self-exile which God himself undergoes. He who once filled the universe retreats from part of that universe. The reasons for this are complex and varied. One of the more obvious reasons, which Scholem explains in his book *On The Kabbalah and Its Symbolism*, is that the limitation creates a "pneumatic, primordial space ... and makes possible the existence of something other than God and His pure essence."

From this exiled position, the *Shekinah* (God's visage; His radiance) sends forth its ray of light into the primordial space where creation takes place. One form creation takes is *Adam Kadmon*, or Primordial Man, whose eyes refract the lights of creation emanating from the *Shekhinah*. This holy radiance is to be refracted into vessels consisting of lower mixtures of light. Upon impact, however, these vessels are shattered. Scholem states, "This is the decisive crisis of all divine created being, the 'breaking of the

Crackpot: A Lurianic Myth

vessels';" after this event, the heaviest sparks and portions of the broken vessel fall to lead an existence of their own as daemonic powers.

The result is devastating: a myth of alienation and redemption is created. Scholem states, "After this crisis nothing remains as it was. Everything is somewhere else. But a being not in its proper place is in exile. Thus, all being is in need of redemption."

Everything is flawed, like the female hunchback and the blind man who create Hoda, like the bodies of the men who come to her for comfort:

> Sometimes they were indeed horrible deformities of the human vessel ... often they were such little things, such minor cracks andchips and variations in the human design ... In the minutest flaw men divined perfection withheld, and saw them selves cast down.

Hoda herself knows that she is a cracked vessel. Though she is called a "sturdy little vessel" early in the novel, she is destined to break for her father has "stolen the brightness from the sun," the *Shekhinah's radiance*, which is rumoured to have caused his blindness. This brightness, or "sweetness," accounts for Hoda's love, compassion, joy, and sensitivity, by which she attempts to spread good will and comfort throughout the miserable, dark world about her. But these qualities, mixed with her own imperfections (for instance, her early ignorance of how babies are made), result in a painful series of events that at times bring her to the brink of madness.

Early in the novel, Danile, who is referred to as a "leaky vessel," reveals to Hoda his own perception of the Lurianic universe:

> I don't know; it's hard to figure it all out. There seems to be somthing not quite altogether between time and place and feelings and events. The pieces don't match up; they won't hold, the right time, the right place in life, the right feeling, the right length and strength for each ... there are just too many pieces, each reaching for the others, and each being swept along in a different direction.

It takes Hoda some time to accept this vision. Essentially she is an optimist, a reveler, a girl who celebrates everyone's wedding and weeps at everyone's funeral. Her concerns are universal. It is rumoured she even visits the gentile cemetery. She says she feels like "a direct tap to the source of boundless good will, just waiting to be turned on." Given Hoda's future occupation, the "turned on" may be too heavy a pun; yet it must be kept in mind that Hoda makes no moral distinction between sexual and spiritual goodwill. And upon the character of her schoolteacher, Miss Boltholmsup, guardian of WASP squeamishness, prejudice, and Puritanism, Hoda streams forth like a ray of light, revealing the neurotic, paranoid mind that has been given authority over a classroom of children.

No moral consideration of her activities breaks in on Hoda until after she unexpectedly gives birth to a son. The scene is the most vivid in the novel and we are invited to make a connection with the "breaking of the vessel," through the process of birth. Again, creation is imperfect. Reacting spontaneously, Hoda bites the umbilical cord; she ties an unprofessional knot that leaves her son "flawed" and determines his name, *Pipick*, (Yiddish for navel).

From this point on, Hoda must contend with her guilt (she anonymously leaves the child on the steps of an orphanage), a guilt which drives her at times to think of herself "running, sucked by invisible forces through the dark streets."

In Luria's Kabbalistic thinking there is the implication that the exile of the *Shekhinah* may be a symbol for our own guilt. It is therefore fitting that Hoda is now able to catch glimpses of a Lurianic universe. Listening to a story of sexual depravity concerning the director of the orphanage, Hoda thinks of her own life:

> ... something came to life in her, shards of an irrevocable Hoda, buriedall those years in her own flesh, searing through her to a lost wholeness.

She now has "the suspicion that in fact some situations are irremediable," and when the guilt over her orphaned son reaches its zenith, we are told:

Crackpot: A Lurianic Myth

She, who had experienced at times an electrifying sense of the unity of beings, now felt the jagged chill of dislocation, of separation even of herself from herself.

Here we have the keynote to the Lurianic experience — the exile of the self from the self.

In an attempt to alleviate this guilt, Hoda sends anonymous donations to the orphanage for her son, whom she calls "the Prince." Aside from Pipick, he is also called David, which, like "the Prince," has associations with royalty. In the Lurianic myth, the Prince is a messianic figure. This is not Hoda's first prince. Earlier in the novel she indulges in adolescent fantasies of involvement with the Prince of Wales. She leaves a mysterious note with her newborn son, which leads to the baby's royal nickname. The connection here, between Hoda's romantic delusion and her belief in the future success of her offspring, may suggest that her Messianic dream is adolescent in nature.

Luria is very clear on this: *Tikkun*, or redemption from the tragedy of the shattered vessel, requires every Jew to participate in good deeds and prayer. As Scholem states, "In the Lurianic myth the Messiah becomes a symbol ... the coming of the Messiah means no more than a signature under a document that we ourselves write." Like much of Jewish theology, the Lurianic Kabbalah is essentially existential in nature, emphasizing action over dreams.

Not until Hoda gives up her dreams about both Princes is she ready for redemption. She decides it would be detrimental to try to make contact with her now wandering son; we are told, "Hoda no longer nursed futile dreams."

Hoda is not the only messianic believer. Her son seems able to bring out the dreams of the entire community:

> The congregation was much impressed by the piety and sense of responsibility of the foundling son, and dredged up instances from the Holy Works of like special cases who had been mysteriously introduced among the people, to perform eventually feats especially assigned from heaven.

Hoda's son is seen as a "champion, destined to engage and vanquish this new fiend of Europe, this German Hitler." It is also expected that the Prince will eventually be cast out by his own community and made an exile, which is exactly what happens later in the novel when a powerful member of the community, in need of a scapegoat, generates false rumours about David. For Luria tells us that even if the Messiah were to come, we would act like those at Sinai, worshipping the golden calf and casting God's gift aside.

A further aspect of the Lurianic myth which bears relevance to the novel concerns the *Shekhinah* (thought of as feminine) being torn from the Godhead, *Ze'ir* (which is masculine). To make herself whole, Hoda must find a man; a marriage of masculine and feminine must take place. She meets a displaced person named Lazar who has lost his wife and children in the Holocaust. Like Lazarus, he has risen from the dead:

> ... he was plucked alive from all that dead flesh; out of
> all that pile of bodies he alone dragged himself free
> and crawled away from the charred pit.

Hoda originally rejects Lazar because he offers her a "new life," and she is done with such hopes and dreams:

> You know what happened to the last guy went around
> offering new lives? They nailed him up!

But Lazar proves to be strong and sensitive, and Hoda is moved when given a glimpse of his tragic past, which Lazar believes lives eternally in the present; he asks, "How can you remember what can never become the past?" Hoda identifies with Lazar's suffering and yet realizes the enormity of it in comparison to hers. She is shamed and at the same time conquered. In the end, she extends herself towards Lazar, thus existentially returning the feminine to the masculine.

In her final vision, which concludes the novel, Hoda appears to come to terms with her life. We are told, "She occupies her past; she inhabits her life." Her vision takes place in a dream; whether that disrupts the strength of the vision is a matter for speculation. All one can say is that Hoda sees herself participating in a scene of reunification, drawing "a magic circle" around a class of children, telling them that soon "they would all be stirring the muddy waters in the brimming pot together."

The broken vessel has been mended, and a vision of universal interaction, physical as well as spiritual, is promised.

A. M. KLEIN: BURNT ANGEL

One is tempted to ask whether or not there would be so much interest in A. M. Klein had he not chosen silence over the word. Certainly Klein's work merits the interest in itself, but it is also fair to say that *what happened* to Klein adds another dimension to that interest. He joins that galaxy of poets — Delmore Schwartz, Sylvia Plath, John Berryman — into whose lives we read some myth of the poet in the modern world. In their failures, obsessions, silences, and suicides, we see a key to the significance of the struggle between the sensitive creative individual and society. Their lives become fascinating fictions.

Usher Caplan's *Like One That Dreamed*, is a well put together biography that invites such reading into. Rather than belabouring the details of Klein's life, Caplan weaves a rich tapestry, dealing with major motifs under chapter headings culled from Klein's own works, and juxtaposing poignant selections from Klein's published and unpublished writing with the relevant sections of the biographical text. To his credit, Caplan has not attempted to pin his subject down; what emerges is the unsettled mosaic of A. M. Klein: poet, novelist, politician, lawyer, teacher, editor, speechwriter, logician, rhetorician, and moralist.

While most artists in the modern era have seen themselves as being on the periphery of society, and of the community from which they come, Klein saw himself as integral to it — as one of its leading spokesmen. Unlike James Joyce, his literary hero, Klein could not accept the fact that the community at large is almost always indifferent to and often inimical towards art. He found it difficult to accept and live by the fact that the serious poet in contemporary societies is more often than not the outcast, outlaw, and pariah. Klein's uneasiness in dealing with that role of the poet was partly a result of his temperament, partly a result of his closeness to the immigrant experience in the New World.

There is a wonderful scene in the film *Hester Street* in which a quiet, sensitive man, a Talmudic scholar back in Europe, is seated at a sewing machine in a turn of the century New York City sweatshop. The wealthy factory owner — a loud-mouthed boor who, back in the old country, eked out a living as a rag peddler — is seen pacing before the rows of sweating faces. He suddenly recognizes the scholar; it seems they come from the same village back home. "Some country, America," the owner says, slapping his belly and laughing maliciously his gold capped teeth glinting. "Some country. Back home I was da peddler and misteh scholar here looked down his nose at me. Now, I look down my nose at him. Some country."

Compare that scene with this psychologically telling passage that Caplan provides from one of Klein's unpublished novels. Note the influence of the narrator's mother, her role as representative of the New World values:

> Lately, when I would sit in my red rep chair, engrossed in a book, valet to some statesman, or poet, or buccaneer, I would suddenly raise my head, and surprise her, presumably in the act of knitting, watching me. The doleful expression on her never particularly joyful face — tears upon parchment — at once saddened and enraged me. I knew what that expression meant — it was criticism: once he was so full of promise and hope, and now, look at him, blighted, ambitionless, a reader of books. Like the rest of them he might have been, only more successful, a buyer of fur-coats for his mother, a car-owner, a proprietor — instead, distorted values had steered him away from what was rightfully his.[1]

Klein could not break from his community as Joyce broke from his. As a result, he spent his life torn between an image of himself as poet and individual, and as member of his race, his community. He lived between two worlds: the world of the past, which he romanticized, and the contemporary world, which he found morally and spiritually bankrupt. One might guess from reading Klein's poetry that he was a devout Jew, or at least a practising one. Caplan reveals he was neither. Rather, he was a die-hard sentimentalist about tradition, about what he termed "his folk." This sentimentality made it difficult for him to see the community for what it was and to accept his true status in it. When he finally did admit to what it was, he wrote his finest poem, "Portrait of the Poet as Landscape." It is interesting to note, however, that even in that poem Klein does not express the anger and bitterness that one might expect from such a realization. The poem is written in the third person and as the title indicates, it is a portrait, what you look at from a distance.

Klein is himself one of the "schizoid solicitudes" he refers to in that monumental poem. Schizoid in the real sense of meaning split — between his self and his community, between his more creative impulses and his desire to represent that community and be accepted by it. It is that latter side we see in Klein the U.J.A. fund raiser, in Klein the speech-writer for Sam Bronfman, head of Seagram's; it is also the side most revealed in the pieces that comprise *Beyond Sambation: Selected Essays and Editorials 1928-1955*, the first in a series of the collected works of Klein by U. of T. Press. The series is an admirable project; this, however, is an unfortunate volume to start with. Most of the selections were written for the *Canadian Jewish Chronicle*. In his biography, Caplan claims the significance of these editorials: "Klein's term of editorship coincided with the most terrible (i.e. the holocaust) and most glorious (the birth of the state of Isreal) years in modern Jewish history. In his empathic sensitivity to the events of those years, Klein spoke personally for a nation."

True. And all of Klein's sentiments are appropriate: he deplores Hitler and Mussolini; he sees Stalin early on for the hypocritical tyrant he was; he takes the Canadian government to task over its treatment of Japanese Canadians during W.W. II; he calls for understanding in dealing with Arab refugees from Palestine. All the right sentiments. And that's exactly what puts one off.

A.M. Klein: Burnt Angel

One might not go so far as Klein's contemporary, the poet Leo Kennedy, who, during the forties, worked for an ad agency. He wrote to Klein: "Those editorials in the *Chronicle*, Abe, are even lower than my copywriting." But the point is well taken.

On the positive side, Klein displays in these essays a very sharp analytical mind. He is very good at taking apart the argument of an anti-Semite or a Jewish apologist. Many of the parts that make up the section "Notebook of a Journey" based on his trip to Israel and Europe are effective because they are more the work of an itinerant journalist than that of a self-conscious editorialist.

On the negative side, Klein's biblical rhetoric is hard to take for any extended period of time. His sentimentality is schmaltzy, his style often rococo. He is passionate, humanitarian, yet somehow uninteresting. He is always waving a moral banner. He is so good that one often feels he does not belong to this century. Like one of the angels in his well-known poem, "A Psalm of Abraham, Concerning That Which He Beheld Upon The Heavenly Scarp," Klein is always gazing down on man from above. There is no indication that he has absorbed the impact of such thinkers as Freud, Kafka, Kierkegaard, or Nietzsche. In fact, in one of the essays in this collection he refers to Nietzsche as a nineteenth-century decadent. Klein does not feel tainted and hence he displays, in his published work at least, little if any self-introspection, no psychological awareness. He is generally dealing with an outmoded vision of man.

To understand Klein more fully it is interesting to compare him to another Jewish North American poet of the same generation, Delmore Schwartz. Schwartz, like Klein, became a casualty of the struggle between the poet and North American society. Like Klein he too came from the immigrant class and was susceptible to the same extreme pressures of "making it." One of the differences, however, was that early on in his career, Schwartz addressed the tensions inherent in the role of the modern poet. The following are passages from two of his essays:

> He (the modern poet) does feel that he is a stranger, an alien, an outsider; he finds himself without a father or mother, or he is separated from them by the opposition between his values as an artist and their values as respectable members of modern

society. This opposition cannot be avoided because not a government subsidy, nor yearly prizes, nor a national academy can disguise the fact that there is no genuine place for the poet in modern life. He has no country, no community, inso far as he is a poet, and his greatest enemy is money, since poetry does not yield him a livelihood.[2]

> The poet, above all is the one who feels the central lack in what men do, know, and believe, because he works in terms of consciousness as in terms of words. We ought to remember that perhaps the greatest evil of capitalism is its oppression or perversion of all values and thus of all lives. . . . And it is in the lives of the most intelligent and the most sensitive that the greatest harm is done, at least to the intelligence and the sensibility.[3]

Schwartz, unlike Klein, was totally tuned into modernity. Part of the reason for this may have been the fact that Schwartz lived south of the border where assimilation into the general rush of culture was quicker and more radical. He was one of the first of the "Manhattan intellectuals"; he was largely responsible for making the term "sensibility" a trade word in sophisticated conversations. His essay topics range from a brilliant explication of the symbolism in Faulkner's *A Fable* to the significance of W. C. Field's comic genius. Klein's notebooks were filled with commentary on Joyce while Schwartz's, according to Robert Lowell, were filled with "notes on Joyce and pornography."[4] Schwartz seemed to thrive on the crosscurrents and contradictions of the modern age. His essays, read today, have a freshness and immediacy that Klein's lack. The essays in *Beyond Sambation* are a cut above your everyday editorial, but far below what one expects from a creative writer of Klein's talent.

During his editorship, Klein received complaints now and then that the language he used in these essays was beyond his readers. Commenting upon this in his introduction to the essays, M.W. Steinberg writes:

> While on the one hand it is to his credit that he never wrote down to his public and that he tried to be himself in his writ-

ing, saying what he had to say in the manner that best suited and pleased himself, these characteristics of his style suggest a measure of intellectual ostentation, and his indifference, insofar as it existed, perhaps indicates an aspect of cultural snobbishness, or at least conscious distancing . . .

The real point here, around which Steinberg is hedging, is that while Klein was perhaps "writing up" in terms of style, in terms of content he was writing *for* his audience. Language, used as ostentatiously as Klein used it, is often an avoidance tactic, a disguise, a way to hide from feeling. Klein's language is impressive, but is it deeply felt? Is it authentic?

How ironic and sad, that after Klein had given up the writing of poetry and fiction, after he had given up his law practice, given up seeing his friends, and entered the terrible silence that filled his final years, he remained on Seagram's payroll list and every year dutifully sent Sam Bronfman a birthday greeting. Perhaps Bronfman was his doppleganger — the man of power, of action, the one "the community" really respected, the one who had "made it."

NOTES

[1] See also Klein's article "Notes on a 'Court Jew'" in *Beyond Sambation*.

[2] "The Isolation of Modern Poetry" from Donald Dike and David Zucker, ed., *Selected Essays of Delmore Schwartz*. (Chicago: The University of Chicago Press, 1970), pp. 9-10.

[3] "Rimbaud In Our Time," from *Selected Essays of Delmore Schwartz*, p. 57.

[4] See Lowell's sonnet for Schwartz in his book, *History*.

ELI MANDEL:
THE FAMILY ROMANCE

Eli Mandel has had an interesting double career. He is not only one of our foremost poets, but also one of our most perceptive literary critics. This recent collection of critical essays (*The Family Romance.* Turnstone Press) will enhance his reputation in that second category.

It is a book that is important for several reasons; three of the major ones I will outline here. Firstly, in two of the pieces, Mandel provides us with some acute insights into his own creative process and helps us to understand the motives and workings of a contemporary poet. Secondly, in essays such as "The Death of the Long Poem" and "Strange Loops", he adeptly describes the present position of literature, the "impossibility", as he terms it, of modernism, and the problematic nature of post-structuralist theory. He provides us with a series of profound speculations on our in-between state, that terrain of creative absence that deconstruction has formed, showing as well, how Canadian literature has developed within this process. And thirdly, Mandel introduces into Canadian critical thought the Freudianism of Harold Bloom, whose brilliant and challenging work, *The Anxiety of Influence,* favourably haunts many of these essays.

Mandel's discussions cover a wide range of topics, but for the purpose of this review I wish to comment on two ontological questions, two problems of identity, which *The Family Romance* raises. One relates to the author's character; the other, to the

Eli Mandel: The Family Romance

nation's.

The most moving pieces in this book are "Auschwitz and Poetry" (a daring title since one would have expected "Auschwitz and Silence") and "The Long Poem: Journal and Origin." Both are autobiographical, both about origins. Each attempts to reveal the process by which a poem is written: the first, through recollection and description; the second from inside the very process of writing, through diary and journal. "Auschwitz and Poetry" is extraordinary in that it not only attempts to account for the origin of a poem under consideration ("On the 25th Anniversary of the Liberation of Auschwitz: Memorial Services, Toronto, January 25, 1970"), but also contains a section about the genesis of the poet, his primary "motive for metaphor."

In this section, Mandel presents himself as a young man who has recently returned from the Second World War. Before him lies the awesome task of visiting his aunt and uncle to tell them of the last moments he spent with his cousin, their soldier son, who was killed in Normandy. Mandel writes: "I was the last of the family to see him alive," thus presenting himself as a witness, a survivor who in Eli Wiesel's words, must "suffer for not having suffered." It is not absurd, in this instance, to think of Mandel's cousin as the poet's projected other, his dead double, his ghost image, and — since poems are litanies against death — as the impetus for the poem Mandel is soon to write. During his odyssey home, Mandel stops over at the house of his dead cousin's sister, where, "On an oppressively hot day, alone in the house, moody, depressed, I picked up a book ..." What he reads are words by Thomas Mann, relating the notion of suffering to creativity: "...certain attainments of the soul and intellect are impossible without disease." That night, Mandel writes his first poem, "Estevan, Saskatchewan", which begins with the line: "A small town bears the mark of Cain." Cain and Abel — the dark doubles. Mandel and his cousin.

Harold Bloom believes that the poet's calling arises from two death anxieties — the fear of physical death as well as a possible poetic death. Mandel's account supports this theory. In the first place, he has seen his own death in the spectre of his cousin; secondly, by picking up Mann's book, he has taken on the long struggle with the giant literary precursors, some of whom he goes on to name: Dostoevsky, Kafka, Joyce. The account also reveals something about the connection between repression and poetry. One might ask why the day was oppressive? Why the poet-to-be was depressed? What did he ever say to his aunt and uncle? He highlights the notion of repression by referring to the Auschwitz poem as "an unsayable poem, a series of inevitable evasions." Poetry then as a swerving, a way of intimating what cannot be said, a way of speaking around. On the personal level there is Mandel, the survivor of his cousin. On the larger historical scale, there is Mandel, a Jew who was exempt from the Shoah, the annihilation of his people. The technical problem Mandel poses is: How does one truly write about an event like Auschwitz, especially if one was not a direct witness? I quote his eloquent response:

> I cannot recall to the day when it occurred to me I had been given a solution ... There was a way to write the poem to be thought of as "Auschwitz." It would be a series of displacements: structurally, grammatically, imagistically, psychologically. It would be a camp poem by not being a camp poem. Stuttering. All theatricality. All frantic posturing. All pointing to a resolution that would not be a resolution, a total ambiguity in which two different moments (Toronto 1970 Estevan 1930) dissolved into one another seamlessly, becoming at that instant another time, the unimaginable place of the killing ground itself.

"Auschwitz and Poetry" ends with the now established poet visiting the Dachau death camp and prophesying that he will one day "be writing about this moment." This leads to Mandel's essay "The Long Poem: Journal and Origin." Here Mandel is flying to Russia, returning to an earlier origin than Estevan, namely, to the home of his father and his father's father. On his return trip he will visit Dachau and Munich where he will witness the carnival of Fasching and will be told by a fellow Jewish writer that the ritual is named after "sticks, bundles of sticks. As in the fasches, in 'fascist'. The sticks were used to beat the old Jews who were driven through the lines of revellers." This revelation leads Mandel to an epiphany:

Eli Mandel: The Family Romance

> I think of the theatrical carnival of fasching in Munich, and the ultimate theatre of cruelty nearby, in a little German town, and of all the old Jews whipped through holiday streets, of the Dnieper and Mother Russia where the same pograms were acted out, and I wonder at what dark impulse took me one day onto that Aeroflot to the Soviet World so that I could see its shadowy images and the ancient play acted still one more time.

The piece concludes with a quotation from Freud, which, given the passage that precedes it, strikes the reader as dreadful in its irony: "Instinctual repression (is) a measure of the level of civilization that has been reached."

Mandel has always displayed an uncanniness in his ability to relate the general social-political malaise to his own inner drama. This is what accounts for the power of his book *Life Sentence*, a collection of poems and diary entries whose theme is betrayal – betrayal experienced on a personal level and perceived in the wider political sphere. But in the two pieces discussed above, it seems to me that Mandel has proceeded deeper into his uncanniness for he has arrived at the terrifying probability that repression is not only at the source of art, but also at the source of historical cruelty. Hence, Auschwitz *and* poetry. It is a position arrived at by others, no doubt, but in these autobiographical pieces we find it expressed in a particlarly powerful manner: "the theatrical carnival of fasching and the ultimate theatre of cruelty nearby," referring simultaneously to the Dachau camp and to Antonin Artaud's Theatre of Cruelty. And here we might recall the quotation I provided from the first piece where Mandel reveals that his poem on Auschwitz will be "all theatrically." To complete this ironic circle — what Mandel refers to as a "strange loop" — we should point out that it is the awareness of connections such as those we have just described that has helped to undermine the project of Western civilization, and has caused the very crisis in literature that Mandel's book describes.

I wish to move on to my second question of identity which is national in scope and which arises from a comment Mandel makes in his preface. But first, a brief synopsis of Harold Bloom's theory, which, as stated before, informs much of this book. According to Bloom, every new poet must mis-read, mis-interpret his strong poet predecessors if his work is to appear unique and if he is to establish his own place in the poetic arena. To use a biblical metaphor — each poet is a Jacob, wrestling with the Angel who can be seen alternatively as the angel of death, or, as the strong poet father. This struggle continues until the poet is victorious and given a new name, a prophetic name. He then takes his rightful place within the tribe of poets. Literature then, is inter-textual; poems are re-visions of earlier poems. This is why literary influence is felt as anxiety provoking. A poet does not simply appear. His or her strength depends upon having struggled with the strong father/mother poets. Which is why young poets often sound like the celebrated poets of a previous generation; they have not yet learned to subvert their influences. It is my contention that this theory of poetry has a special meaning for Canadian culture.

In his preface to the collection under review, Mandel comes close to apologizing for his use of Bloom's theory:

> ... there are other problems raised by this sort of approach to a literary history and some sort of justification should be offered. There is the peculiarity that once again an approach claiming insight into Canadian writing finds its origins in non-Canadian sources. It is tainted by an old dilemma, colonialism.

To my knowledge, Bloom, an American, nowhere in his writings expresses that particular unease felt by Mandel, though he makes extensive use of European thinkers and theorists to develop and apply his critical stance. There are, I think, two reasons for this. Firstly, Bloom perceives his critical roots as being largely French since the father of deconstruction theory is Jacques Derrida. This is in itself a mis-reading since Derrida is, I believe, originally Algerian and his theories are derived for the most part from German thinkers. But historically, Americans like their revolutions — either political or cultural — to originate in the land of the stormed Bastille. Secondly, and more importantly, Bloom has his own, that is, American deconstructionist ghost to support his vision —namely, Emerson.

Mandel's uneasiness can be explained by the fact that there is no comparable ghost in Canadian letters. As Earle Birney put it in his poem "Can Lit": "it's only by our lack of ghosts/we're haunted." I would alter that to say that we have our ghosts — Bliss Carman, Charles G. D. Roberts, Lampman — but unfortunately they cannot compete with the terrible presence of Melville, Poe, Whitman. In fact, the true meaning of colonialism in its cultural sense now becomes clear: the swallowing of one nation's ghosts by the more powerful ghosts of another. But modern Canadian poets must be commended, for if the poets of Birney's generation came upon a scene lacking in strong precursors, that is surely no longer the case. The fact is, to the present generation of Canadian poets, Purdy, Layton, Cohen, Atwood, and Ondaatje, have all proved to be significant influences. And whether these poets chose as their models American or European influences seems to me to be beside the point. As Mandel states: "where there was emptiness, there are now words."

Yet our concern over the "emptiness," and our obsession with the metaphysical absence — what Northrop Frye terms "the wilderness" — persists. If Bloom is correct in seeing modern creativity as a problem of the anxiety of influence, then Mandel has performed an essential task by injecting this critical concept into our literary bloodstream. I believe it can provide us with a more dynamic reading of our own literature, as evidenced by Mandel's brilliant essay on the novels of Hugh MacLennan, which, of all his considerations of other writers, applies Bloom's type of thinking most strenuously.

As a postscript I will say that it now seems to me that we Canadians have displayed a fine uncanniness in our relentless obsession with this question of identity. All along we may have been acting the role of deconstruction's true masters of absence. "A Canadian," wrote Irving Layton, "is someone who goes from one coast to the other gravely asking 'What is a Canadian?'" A statement tinged with sarcasm but bespeaking its own, perhaps unintended, seriousness. For in our late arriving, in our coming after the fact, in our struggle with "colonial mentality", who, more than we, know the anxiety of influence?

MIRIAM WADDINGTON:
APARTMENT SEVEN

Miriam Waddington's prose has much in common with her poetry. The language is direct and lucid; the voice is open and personal. The style stems from her conviction that literature has the power to communicate in an immediate way, that it can change lives. The prose collected in *Apartment Seven* differs, however, from her poetry in one significant aspect — it is charged with a polemic, one which informs practically each of the various essays, critiques and reminiscences that comprise this book and which raises it from being merely good to being important.

Waddington's polemic comes out of her belief that there is a suppressed tradition of writing in Canada. Her essay, "Canadian Tradition and Canadian Literature" is central to an understanding of her argument. In it she outlines the history of our literary attitudes and points to the ongoing attempt by critics to describe what they have perceived as a dualism in our literature. Waddington admits it is difficult to pinpoint what that dualism is though she seems certain of what it is not. She dismisses, for example, A. J. M. Smith's division of our writers into "native" and "cosmopolitan." There is, of course, something reductive about any such division for genuine writers and writing in general resist such simplifications. Waddington seems aware of this. Yet for argument's sake she provides her own dichotomy, dividing our critical attitudes into the mythopoeic-apocalyptic (i.e., Northrop Frye) on the one hand, and the historical socio-economic (i.e., E. K. Brown) on the other. This dichotomy permits Waddington to make her point: namely, that the mythopoeic school has held the upper hand in defining our tastes and as a result the literature of our poor, native, and ethnic populations has not had the reception it deserves. Her claim is that the real and specific events of our past are denied by a patterned, mythic approach to literature. She concludes her essay by questioning the very notion of a Canadian tradition and in so doing, provides what I believe is a true and telling account of our literary situation:

> There is, in fact, no real Canadian literary tradition but only a social matrix, an accumulation of historical events, full of contradictions, forces and counter-forces; we live in a sort of vast cultural chaos upon which all are free to draw. We possess a promiscuous history, which contains not just abstract patterns, but specific items.

What Waddington is engaged in here is not merely an academic debate to be carried on by professors at a conference. She is attempting to talk about how our culture and society operate at the deepest levels, and what lends her argument weight is the fact that it is born out of her personal experience. From childhood, Waddington has felt herself an outsider in Canadian society, estranged because she is both a woman and a Jew. In her memoir pieces she describes her roots in the secular Jewish immigrant culture, a culture strongly socialist and humanistic. This genesis accounts for her sensitivity to those artists, groups, and works that have been disenfranchised or considered *déclassé* by our commissars of culture. Those essays in *Apartment Seven* which are most significant are so because they perform the act of reclaiming forgotten or unknown works, of reaching out to what Waddington so eloquently terms, "the denied realities."

There is, for instance, the persuasive essay on the early radical poems of A. M. Klein which have been ignored or dismissed by critics as being immature, without literary value, representing a "troubling episode in an otherwise virtuous literary life." Waddington argues convincingly that these political poems are organically connected to Klein's later work and are not an aberration; they are, rather, a fascinating record of how a Canadian poet responded to the revolutionary thirties and moreover, are "still fresh, interesting, and alive."

The piece on Rachel Korn, the Montreal Yiddish poet whom Waddington has translated over the years, is particularly valuable for it will serve, for the majority of Canadian readers, as an introduction to a dynamic and major poet. (As proof for such a claim, one has only to read Korn's "The Beginning of a Poem," quoted in full in Waddington's essay. I can think of no other work that speaks so well to Akhmatova's notion of "pre-lyrical anxiety," the terrifying nature of the creative surge.)

Two of the most fascinating essays are "The Heroes of Misfortune," a study of the central figures in narratives by I. L. Peretz, Lu Hsun and V. S. Naipaul, and "Moshe Nadir: The Yiddish Stephen Leacock." In these, Waddington examines the relationship between authors/characters and the societies they lived in. The essays point to the complex relationship between the writer and his/her culture and help us to appreciate the tensions, motives and aspirations of those on the margins of society.

I found only one of Waddington's acts of reclamation unconvincing and that was her piece on the poetry of John Sutherland. I find Sutherland's language static, bulky, and somehow oppressive; I left the essay feeling that Irving Layton had been right in dissuading him from the poet's vocation. Also, Waddington's "feminist" essays, "Bias" and "Women and Writing" are tepid: their ideas, old hat. She is much better on women's issues when she writes about specific female writers. The pieces on Simone de Beauvoir and Mary Wollstonecraft are inclusive and thought provoking.

Waddington's contention of a suppressed literature is nowhere better expressed than in her essay on Hugh Garner's *Cabbagetown* and in her "Memoirs of a Jewish Farmer: Edenbridge." The latter deals with Michael Usishkin's recollections of the turn-of-the-century socialist pioneering settlement in Saskatchewan. It is apparent from the lengthy passages Waddington quotes that Usishkin's book is as fascinating and well written as, say, Susanna Moodie's *Roughing It In the Bush*. Though Waddington does not pose the question, one is tempted to ask: On how many CanLit courses will you find Usishkin's book? Which leads to a more pressing question. For if we indeed see ourselves in and through our literature, then what effects have we suffered by ignoring or denying parts of that literature?

Waddington sees Hugh Garner's *Cabbagetown* as another neglected book which critics have condemned as didactic and aesthetically weak. Through an examination of Garner's use of language, Waddington proves otherwise. Here the suppressed minority is not an ethnic group but the desperately poor. Turning back to her polemic, Waddington wonders how placing this novel in a larger mythic framework would "enlarge our experience?" She concludes the essay by referring to the hard-won hopefulness of *Cabbagetown's* protagonist, then goes on to expose what she sees as the underlying politics of the mythopeic school:

> What's important, and what our conservative cultural critics and tastemakers want us to lose in a welter of mythic translation, is the particular, the specific past. To make of myth such a weighty influential criterion is not only to undervalue the specific past, but it is also to deny the present, and to fear the future. Although the term future is an abstract concept, its equivalent in psychological terms is hope. . . hope is dangerous: inciting it in others may lead them to act . . . No wonder realism is out of fashion.

Not only realism, but humanism as well. For that is what other poets in this tradition have attempted to do — humanize Canadian culture. That is why Irving Layton has often condemned our literature as "saurian," as cold, reserved, genteel. A. M. Klein might have put it this way — pay attention to people, not *paysage*.

Waddington has paid close attention to people. A poet leaves her biological family and adopts a literary one. Waddington provides us with a loving portrait of her literary mother, the poet Ida Maza. As already mentioned, she writes with feeling and depth on the works of her literary father, A. M. Klein. There are fine recollections of Dorothy Livesay and Raymond Souster, and a touching portrait of the spinster sisters, Birdie and Angela with whom Waddington boarded as a university student.

In a decade where strident feminist rhetoric and scientific argot pass for poetry, where post-structuralist and deconstructionist theories abound, Waddington's humanism and commitment to experience seem salutary. By reclaiming outcast writing, she has extended our collective memories and broadened the gamut of voices we may hear.

ROBIN SKELTON:
THE EDGE OF TIME

George Woodcock said that Robin Skelton belongs to "the whole of the English poetic tradition." With the publication of this new book we can drop the qualifier, for here Skelton employs, not only English, but classical Greek, Indian, and Welsh poetic forms as well. Each is labelled beneath the title of the poem, with the result that reading through *The Edge of Time* is like walking through a botanical garden: one comes across the *Sextilla*, the *Pantoum*, the incredible *Iambelegus*. Such a stroll is both fascinating and frustrating. A reader of poetry may be curious about the tradition of the art and interested in seeing how these forms are worked. Classifying them, however, removes them from the wilds, from that region of spontaneity where we believe poetry thrives. Yet it is significant that amidst the present deluge of "poetry" books, many of them collections of tepid prose fragments, Skelton has brazenly provided us with this compendium of poetic form.

In this century there has been an ongoing debate about the usefulness of traditional prosody. We can take rhyme as an example. Some believe that in searching for a rhyme to fit a regular metered pattern, a poet will be led to uncharted linguistic and intellectual regions. After all, most of us think in a predetermined manner and would choose a predictable word or phrase to express an idea, experience, or emotion. Rhyme can lead us away from our banality, and the stress of rhymes, the confluence of certain unexpected words, may suggest unusual comparisons and connections in the reader's mind. There is a playfulness to rhyme, a calling back to childhood. And there is something magical about the repetition of sounds; one can suddenly hear significant echoes in the dull forest of common verbiage. Rhyme also re-establishes the ancient kinship between poetry and music. In an essay entitled "Rhyming on the Counterattack," Primo Levi praised rhyme because it assists memory so that "poems can be transported." One understands the significance of this for one who endured Auschwitz, in part, by recalling cantos from *The Inferno*.

The modern argument *against* rhyme is that it forces us to find a word different from the one we want to use and therefore carries us away from the reality we wish to express. Never before in our culture has there been such an injunction for poets to give voice to the Real. Confronted by Western civilization's destructiveness and hypocrisy, poets early in this century began to challenge the authority of established prosody in an honest attempt to confront the horrors of the age. Tradition can impede that attempt: a poet working with the sonnet form has the entire history of well-known sonnets speaking to him and is liable to sound a chord already heard, one which gave voice to the reality of a different time, a different place.

There is no doubt that this turning away from traditional prosody has done good. One thinks of the best poets of this century who have broken with their culture's traditional poetic forms: Cavafy, Montale, William Carlos Williams, Paz. And yet this exploding of form has reached a point where anyone writing a sonnet is in danger of being considered naïve, or a parodist. In addition, the open form of poetry is now so pervasive that it has become predictable. And the chatty, brother-in-the-street voices of so many contemporary poets are indistinguishable from one another.

In some sense the entire debate about traditional form is somewhat off the mark, for the truth of the matter is that a genuine poet can work effectively with or without it. So long as a poem arises from a dynamic response to reality it will be fresh and convincing, regardless of whether the poet uses established patterns; otherwise, it will be as stuffed and stale as the work of a taxidermist. Furthermore, all successful poems achieve form. The question is what process is used to get there.

Allen Ginsberg, speaking of his poem *Howl*, claims that certain passages have rhythms that "might correspond to classical Greek or Sanskrit prosody." But he emphasizes that he got there "organically rather than synthetically." As he puts it, "The difference is between someone sitting down to write a poem in a definite preconceived metrical pattern and filling in that pattern and someone working with his physiological movements and arriving at a pattern... Nobody's got any objection to iambic pentameter if it comes from the breathing and the belly and the lungs."

Ginsberg here is alluding to Whitman's claim that the poet writes with his body, a fact that most poets would acknowledge. Nevertheless the poetic process is somewhat different for poets who choose from the outset to work with traditional patterns. Their task — and it is an extremely difficult one — is not to surrender to form, but to take it over. Poets who go this route can achieve a formidable tension between the historical baggage carried by form and the contemporary sensibility that speaks through it. Berryman (in *The Dream Songs*) and Lowell (in *History*) spoke convincingly of the here and now through their respective sonnet sequences. As Louise Bogan remarked of Baudelaire (a revolutionary who made extensive use of traditional forms): "When poets put new wines in old bottles, the bottles become new, too."

So we arrive at the critical question whether the forms in Skelton's book have been made anew. Are we being presented with acrostics and parlor tricks, or with poems that emit a voice of life?

It is difficult to give a simple answer. Certainly there are a number of authentic poems here. The majority of these are convincing because they issue from a poet nearing the end of his journey, standing, as the book's title suggests, at the edge of time. For Skelton, time is cyclical. In many of the book's better poems ("The Road Ahead," "Night Blossom In April," "Verse on a Birthday"), the poet predicts his transformation and return, a more romantic view than that of another formalist, Philip Larkin, who approaching his end described death as "the anaesthetic from which none come round." Skelton's title also carries a suggestion of *fin de siècle*; there is an attempt in the structure of the book to link the end of the poet's time with the century's. The second last sequence in the book "A Torn House," contains political poems, most of which seem divorced from Skelton's deeper spiritual concerns. For the most part they are comprised of stock phrases ("hearts gentle and at peace") and worn metaphors ("deaths of children choke the air").

Such weaker poems (and there are, unfortunately several, due partly to the length of the book — 153 pages) remind us that formal structures and traditional echoes can often drown out the individual voice of a poet. In the poem "Her Beauty," for instance, we read:

> *she is as beautiful as time*
> *when lovers murmur*
> *under the trees by the river*
> *where white swans gather.*

Is it possible to write about love and swans and not be overpowered by Yeats?

At his best, Skelton is able to use the poetic pattern as an incantation that leads to metaphysical speculations. We see this in such poems as "Speaking of Grass," "Downfall," "The Return," or the aforementioned "Night Blossom In April" where a flowering cherry tree at night

> *...has renamed night*
> *has redefined the light*
> *made black more black and white*
> *more white than white can be;*
> *its presence urges me*
> *to burn bright as the tree*

My feeling is that today we demand more than mystical incantation or shamanism from out poets. We demand that they help to define man in such perplexing times when horizons continue to shift and the spiritual is suspect. Skelton attempts this in the short sequence entitled "Indian Interlude" and in the poem "In The Museum" where garish city streets are compared to the static, compassionate figures found behind glass. But often, his language is transparent and does not fold back upon itself; there is a lack of contradictoriness, and hence a lack of tension. The lyricism is too pleased with itself and the poet's mystical conclusions, too easily won.

Yet his craftsmanship serves him well in the last section of the book, "*Translations.*" He is certainly one of our finest translators of poetry (see his justly acclaimed renderings of George Faludy's work). Here we have superlative versions of Baudelaire, Apollinaire, and the Russian poet, Yuli Daniel. Skelton is to be praised for bringing these various voices into our lives.

GEORGE FALUDY:
OH, LUCKY MAN

George Faludy is a lucky man. Censored and threatened by the fascists, imprisoned and tortured by the communists, he has lived the sort of life that gives a poet the "voice of authority."

Faludy is fortunate in another sense as well, having had the assistance of very talented translators. In the case of *Selected Poems 1933 – 80*, Robin Skelton has achieved something remarkable as overall editor and as translator of a major portion of the work. A consistent voice runs throughout Faludy's poems; most importantly, they come across as living art rather than as academic exercises. The same level of excellence can be claimed for Kathleen Szasz's translation of Faludy's autobiography, *My Happy Days In Hell*.

It is interesting to read the two volumes, one after the other, since the poems, arranged chronologically, are also a type of autobiography. They chronicle the poet's emotional and intellectual life from his early days in Hungary, through his exile during the Nazi regime, to his emigration to North America.

Faludy spent the first part of the war years in Paris; he then lived in Morocco and later in the United States where he served in the military. After the war, he returned to a "liberated" Hungary, where, as a poet in conflict with the totalitarian state, he was eventually imprisoned. The autobiography concludes with his release from prison while the poems portray his second coming to America.

George Faludy: Oh, Lucky Man

Faludy's persona is large, vibrant, and sensual. A comparable poetic figure in Canadian Literature would be Irving Layton. Like Layton, Faludy is drawn to satire (see especially his attacks on Sartre, Mayakovsky, Milton). His voice is prophetic and moral but swings freely to the erotic:

> *I stared at the thick hair upon her crotch;*
> *velvet black, it grew up to her navel,*
> *and hidden in it what I loved so much*
> *("To Celia, My Faithless Love")*

Faludy also resembles Layton in the way his work exhibits a wide technical range and versatility: he is comfortable with the ballad, the sonnet, the short epigram, and the narrative poem. In terms of craft, he is a traditionalist. He attacks, in the poem entitled "Petronius"

> *the poets and sculptors*
> *who were seeking new modes of expression*
> *with nothing at all novel to express*

It is worthwhile to compare Faludy to other East European poets, to Czechoslovakia's Holub and Seifert, or to Poland's Herbert and Milosz. Faludy is more lyrical, lush, garrulous and romantic. There is a sparseness, a laconic nature to the work of those other East Europeans, perhaps a greater and deeper despair. For despite what Faludy has lived through and all the dark places he has been, he has never surrendered his simple joy in existence. In this aspect he reminds one of the Russian poet Mandelstam who during his exile in Voronezh wrote of the joy in daily pleasures, the beauty of the goldfinch. In Hungary's Recsk prison in the early fifties, Faludy used a number of mental tactics to survive, not the least of which was a delight in simple things: autumn leaves, sunsets, storytelling. His approach to these was not sentimental; rather, they served as an antidote to the horror and ugliness that surrounded him. He also warded off madness by conjuring his childhood memories and by composing long poems in his head (paper and pen were forbidden). What gave him strength was the desire to have these poems survive; in fact, *their* survival was more important to him than his own, which is one of the reasons he recited them to his fellow inmates in the hope that they too may learn them by heart. All of this, because the survival of the poems meant a victory for art, civilization, liberal humanism, over the dull barbarians, whether they be communists, fascists or materialists.

Had history not impinged upon Faludy, he may have developed into a latter day Donne, for his earliest pieces are modern-metaphysical love poems whose themes are expanded and strengthened in the later sonnets (see especially "Death of a Chleuch Dancer" and "Morocco").

What history did was create a more pressing concern for Faludy, perhaps a more political one. The great theme of both the poems and the autobiography is the survival of art, beauty, and love under the onslaught of the ideologues. In various ways, Faludy tells us that the task of man in the modern world is to live without ideology. In his poem "To My Newborn Son," he asks

> *ought he to live like me*
> *without a theory in the centre of the jungle of reality . . .*

In the brilliant piece already referred to, "Petronius", the Roman poet is praised because

> *He created gaiety, radiance, beauty,*
> *although he knew the columns of the dark*
> *were already blocking gates and doors.*
> *I envy him because he did not shudder,*
> *didn't spout heroics, didn't wail . . .*
> *He only made demands upon himself,*
> *not on mankind or on the moves of history,*
> *being so much wiser, so much stronger*
> *than we febrile moderns . . .*

In "Sonnet Ninety-Five (Taoism III)," a world of love and nature, beauty and meditation, is strikingly contrasted to the barbarism and cruelty of ideologues:

George Faludy: Oh, Lucky Man

> I imagine us living like this on the blue-peaked mountain
> ... sitting in meditation,
> loving ...
>
> With you I'd watch the silver-pink fog-snakes writhing ...
> and the green dragons with mouths of silver sipping
> the waterfall and there we'd stroll, or, rather
>
> not, for the mountain is Mao's; his troops arrived
> and shot the monks or buried them alive.

A similar theme runs through *My Happy Days In Hell.* Faludy's autobiography stands in the same league as Nadezhda Mandelstam's *Hope Against Hope, Czeslaw* Milosz's *The Captive Mind* and Milan Kundera's *The Book of Laughter and Forgetting,* all of which depict the struggle of humanism to survive the vicious movements of our century.

Ostensibly, *My Happy Days In Hell* is divided into five parts: France, Africa, The U.S.A. And The People's Democracy, Arrest, The Forced-Labour Camp — but really the book has two major sections. Parts one and two are comprised of reminiscences of childhood in Hungary, and youthful exile in Paris and Morocco. These sections are enchanting and read more like a novel than like an autobiography. Faludy actually uses the word "picaresque" to describe his life during those earlier periods and there are several references to *Don Quixote.* Throughout these early sections, Faludy displays a powerful gift for description as well as a fine ability for drawing characters.

The last three parts of the book make up the second section, which is more strictly autobiographical, and less given to the delight and freedom of the imagination. This is understandable since in this second section a totalitarian regime is attempting to suffocate the poet's soul. The juxtaposition of these two sections gives the book its power and profundity.

This dichotomous structure is evident, in microcosm, from the beginning of the book. Section one presents Faludy as a young boy travelling with Laszlo Fényes, the righteous reporter and defender of the poor (a Quixote figure) who is set against Simon Pan, the boisterous, colourful, depraved and corrupt district administrator. But this is before the age of Stalinism and its colourless bureaucrats, and while Pan is corrupt, he is neither drab nor devoid of charity: he is a realist, politically astute, capable of generosity, while Fényes is the knightly dreamer. Later, in the Paris section, the dichotomies become more a case of "either-or" as evidenced in the philosophical dialogues between Faludy and Bandi. The former argues for a vision of man *sans* ideology; the latter argues for a world under the dictates of communism.

The "Africa" chapter of the book reads like an Arabian tale filled with passion and mystery. It is Morocco's rawness, and anarchistic sensuality that entices Faludy and which repulses his communist friend, Bandi, who despises the place for its lack of order. Later, upon leaving Morocco for the U.S., Faludy regrets departing from a world that he says "fitted my character like a glove." The Africa chapter marks the major division between the two sections of the book and provides us with an articulation of Faludy's deepest concerns:

> My pleasure in Morocco was enhanced to no little degree by the twofold discovery that I had escaped from the increasingly demanding, increasingly disciplined and unbearable workshop of technical civilization and, at the same time, rid myself of certain problems and dilemmas raised by my conscience . . ..
>
> In Morocco, a few moments before the last, victorious onslaught of conquistador civilization, I had a glimpse of the world in which I should have liked to live. I could talk to artisans not yet compelled to spend their lives in the service of a machine . . . I knew a world in which they were sorry for motor-car owners instead of envying them, because, at least symbolically, they had cut off their legs and thus left the world of the living, had wrapped themselves in a cloud of dust, isolating themselves from the titillating temptation of whores and lewd boys, the endless variations of chance encounters and conversations; where poems were still recited by minstrels, and where journalists were no more than modest chroniclers of everyday events and did not believe themselves to be lighthouses of history — and light-houses, which, moreover, guide ships in the wrong direction; where I met a more ancient, to

me more familiar form of storytelling which, instead of describing social reality or presenting flesh and bone people, was content to invent immortal fables.

My greatest joy, however, was that I was rid of all political and moral obligations . . . At last I could live the way I wanted: I observed the world, wrote poetry and spent my days in sweet idleness.

The freedom of the poet: yet it must be noted that Faludy's freedom here is due to his being outside of the society he describes. Had he been an integral member he would have found grave infringements upon his freedom. And though he tells us he enjoys eschewing moral and political obligations, his life story tells us something else, for he consistently chooses not to abandon them and in a sense risks his life for them. Not that he does so by being a political activist; rather, it is by being a poet, a nonconformist, a party of one. It is this stance that will so threaten the Hungarian communists in the next three chapters of the book.

What is also interesting in the Morocco passage above is that the two worlds Faludy contrasts are linked to two different types of writing: the detestable anti-human world of technology is represented by journalism, while the world of minstrels and "immortal fables" is represented by poetry. As already suggested, the war going on in this book is not only contained in the philosophical debates and actions between the dogmatists and the poet but, in a more complex sense, it is being waged on an aesthetic level.

After the war, Faludy decides to leave the U.S. and return to Hungary. His decision is based partly on the fact that he has written about democracy for his homeland and feels he ought, therefore, to help put into practice what he has preached. It is also significant that he spends relatively few pages on his life in America, as if that land failed to stimulate his deeper interests. Perhaps this is because America is the extreme of what he refers to as that "unbearable workshop of technical civilization". As one of his friends ironically puts it: if Faludy remains in the U.S. he will kill the poet in himself, while if he returns to Hungary the worst that can happen is that he himself will be killed.

Which is nearly what happens. Faludy is eventually arrested, imprisoned, and starved. In the pages leading up to his arrest, he provides a vivid account of the hostilities and treacheries amongst the various intellectuals and politicos as eventually each falls victim to the reign of terror. Against the communist true believers and those weaker characters who merely spout their theories to survive, against all who suffer from historical amnesia, who display no sensitivity towards art and beauty, Faludy tenaciously holds on to the humanistic values of his classical education:

> I felt that it was the things I had learned in the Latin, Greek and history classes of my school that formed the stumbling-block on which communism foundered . . . The entire Graeco-Roman world rose up against their (the communist's) pompous, dull and bilious life, from their nurseries hung with Stalin's portraits to their colourless and profane funerals, at which their corpses served merely as a pretext for the party secretary to attack Harry Truman in the funeral oration — all through their days steeped in intrigue, wasted in joylessness, in reckless hysteria or neurotic sham calm, without sincerity, sensuousness, walks, revelry, freedom: yes, the entire Graeco-Roman world rose up against them, the blue and serene skies of Homer, the idylls of Theocritus . . . Catullus's erotics . . . the pornographic frescoes and curses preserved on the walls of Pompeii.

Despite Faludy's valiant attempts to keep the dullness and "joylessness" at bay, they do eventually have their effect. Whereas in childhood, and later in Paris and in Morocco, the poet's imagination was free, his instincts vibrant and alive, under arrest he is engaged in a struggle for survival. Again, this struggle is played out in aesthetic terms. There is an extremely poignant moment in the last part of the book where Faludy's fellow inmates relate the reasons for their arrests. The tales are without exception absurd, almost unbelievable (one youth, for instance, is sent to prison for drinking in the company of those singing outlawed soldier songs). After relating these tales, Faludy has the realization that they are all "utterly uninventable". He goes on to say:

> I thought that these stories would be the main proofs of my

book's authenticity — and this saddened me considerably because until now I always judged books by artistic value and not by authenticity.

It seems to me that this statement heralds an anti-poetic sensibility. It implies a shift in that tension between the authentic and the imaginative, between realism and fantasy, between journalism and poetry. It shifts the balance to the role of the witness.

These are the larger concerns raised by Faludy's life and work — the work, I might add, of a major poet, one of the last writing out of the centre of the European liberal-humanist tradition. And it is just because Faludy writes out of that tradition that some of his poems may fail to strike the contemporary ear as "authentic". I am thinking here of the more blatant satires, such as "Ave Luna, Morituri Te Salutant", or "Letter To The Mayor Of Philadelphia." This is because contemporary poets rarely see themselves as fighters and satirists, as defenders of civilization. Instead of speaking, as a poet like Faludy does, with one foot outside of the swallowing vortex, they now speak in a more halting, fragmented voice from within the vortex. This is especially true of poets in the West. As the critic A. Alvarez points out in his Introduction to the *Selected Poems of Zbigniew Herbert*: "Poets in Western Europe and America react to the cosy, domesticated, senselessly sensible way of life in a mass democracy by asserting the precariousness of things and deliberately exploring the realm of breakdown and madness." It is interesting to speculate what the outcome of such self-absorption will be. My feeling is that Western poets are more threatened than their East European counterparts.

Roland Barthes, in his essay "The Last Happy Writer," makes the point that no one can confidently write satires as Voltaire once did because today we are all engaged in bad faith to a degree that makes it impossible; Barthes believes this is the result of the dreadful events of our century and states, "History has been imprisoned in a difficulty which lacerates any committed literature . . . *no one can any longer give lessons in tolerance to anyone.*" (My italics.) Or, to put it another way, the heart of darkness is in every breast. This is an assumption that has been bought by the majority of Western authors.

It may be true that Faludy's type of struggle is not ours. We might then ask, what is the struggle for a poet living today in Los Angeles or Toronto? Does it have to do with Kierkegaard's phrase about the bourgeois man who tends to "tranquilize himself with the trivial?" Trivialization is a much subtler, less dramatic force than totalitarianism, but it can destroy the human spirit as effectively.

Here and now, people are put to sleep in front of terminal screens, the vast majority of them unaware that a tragedy is taking place. The irony is that democratic nations may serve as the graveyards for art. Those persecuted, exiled writers from the Soviet Bloc and other repressive countries may be the ones who preserve what is essential to great literature since it is in those regimes that literature is still taken seriously: i.e. seen as a dangerous force. Osip Mandelstam, who ultimately died for writing a poem attacking Stalin, once replied to a young poet who was commenting on poetry's lack of popularity: "Why do you complain? Poetry is respected in this country. People are killed for it."

In *this* country, poets are given small government grants, and as Baudelaire put it, "swallowed with a yawn."

Other Books by Kenneth Sherman Published by Mosaic Press

Snake Music
(Mosaic Press, 1978)

The Cost of Living
(Mosaic Press, 1981)

Black Flamingo
(Mosaic Press, 1985)

Relations: Family Portraits
(Mosaic Press, 1986)

Words For Elephant Man
(Mosaic Press, 1983)
Second Printing, 1994

Clusters
(Mosaic Press, 1997)

AGMV MARQUIS
Québec, Canada
1998